Florida Rules of Civil Procedure
2022 Edition

Updated through January 1, 2022

Michigan Legal Publishing Ltd.
QUICK DESK REFERENCE SERIES™

Academic and bulk discounts available at
www.michlp.com

WE WELCOME YOUR FEEDBACK: info@michlp.com

ISBN-13: 978-1-64002-121-1

Table of Contents

Rule 1.010 Scope and Title of Rules

These rules apply to all actions of a civil nature and all special statutory proceedings in the circuit courts and county courts except those to which the Florida Probate Rules, the Florida Family Law Rules of Procedure, or the Small Claims Rules apply. The form, content, procedure, and time for pleading in all special statutory proceedings shall be as prescribed by the statutes governing the proceeding unless these rules specifically provide to the contrary. These rules shall be construed to secure the just, speedy, and inexpensive determination of every action. These rules shall be known as the Florida Rules of Civil Procedure and abbreviated as Fla.R.Civ.P.

Rule 1.020 Privacy and Court Records

Every pleading or other paper filed with the court shall comply with Florida Rule of Judicial Administration 2.425.

Rule 1.030 Nonverification of Pleadings

Except when otherwise specifically provided by these rules or an applicable statute, every pleading or other document of a party represented by an attorney need not be verified or accompanied by an affidavit.

Rule 1.040 One Form of Action

There shall be one form of action to be known as "civil action."

Rule 1.050 When Action Commenced

Every action of a civil nature shall be deemed commenced when the complaint or petition is filed except that ancillary proceedings shall be deemed commenced when the writ is issued or the pleading setting forth the claim of the party initiating the action is filed.

Rule 1.060 Transfers of Actions

(a) **Transfers of Courts**. If it should appear at any time that an action is pending in the wrong court of any county, it may be transferred to the proper court within said county by the same method as provided in rule 1.170(j).
(b) **Wrong Venue**. When any action is filed laying venue in the wrong county, the court may transfer the action in the manner provided in rule 1.170(j) to the proper court in any county where it might have been brought in accordance with the venue statutes. When the venue might have been laid in 2 or more counties, the person bringing the action may select the county to which the action is transferred, but if no such selection is made, the matter shall be determined by the court.
(c) **Method**. The service charge of the clerk of the court to which an action is transferred under this rule shall be paid by the party who commenced the action within 30 days from the date the order of transfer is entered, subject to taxation as provided by law when the action is determined. If the service charge is not paid within the 30 days, the action shall be dismissed without prejudice by the court that entered the order of transfer.

Rule 1.061 Choice of Forum

(a) **Grounds for Dismissal**. An action may be dismissed on the ground that a satisfactory remedy may be more conveniently sought in a jurisdiction other than Florida when:
(1) the trial court finds that an adequate alternate forum exists which possesses jurisdiction over the whole case, including all of the parties;
(2) the trial court finds that all relevant factors of private interest favor the alternate forum, weighing in the balance a strong presumption against disturbing plaintiffs' initial forum choice;
(3) if the balance of private interests is at or near equipoise, the court further finds that factors of public interest tip the balance in favor of trial in the alternate forum; and

   (4)   the trial judge ensures that plaintiffs can reinstate their suit in the alternate forum without undue inconvenience or prejudice.

The decision to grant or deny the motion for dismissal rests in the sound discretion of the trial court, subject to review for abuse of discretion.

(b) **Stipulations in General**. The parties to any action for which a satisfactory remedy may be more conveniently sought in a jurisdiction other than Florida may stipulate to conditions upon which a forum-non-conveniens dismissal shall be based, subject to approval by the trial court. The decision to accept or reject the stipulation rests in the sound discretion of the trial court, subject to review for abuse of discretion.

     A forum-non-conveniens dismissal shall not be granted unless all defendants agree to the stipulations required by subdivision (c) and any additional stipulations required by the court.

(c) **Statutes of Limitation**. In moving for forum-non-conveniens dismissal, defendants shall be deemed to automatically stipulate that the action will be treated in the new forum as though it had been filed in that forum on the date it was filed in Florida, with service of process accepted as of that date.

(d) **Failure to Refile Promptly**. When an action is dismissed in Florida for forum non conveniens, plaintiffs shall automatically be deemed to stipulate that they will lose the benefit of all stipulations made by the defendant, including the stipulation provided in subdivision (c) of this rule, if plaintiffs fail to file the action in the new forum within 120 days after the date the Florida dismissal becomes final.

(e) **Waiver of Automatic Stipulations**. Upon unanimous agreement, the parties may waive the conditions provided in subdivision (c) or (d), or both, only when they demonstrate and the trial court finds a compelling reason for the waiver. The decision to accept or reject the waiver shall not be disturbed on review if supported by competent, substantial evidence.

(f) **Reduction to Writing**. The parties shall reduce their stipulation to a writing signed by them, which shall include all stipulations provided by this rule and which shall be deemed incorporated by reference in any subsequent order of dismissal.

(g) **Time for Moving for Dismissal**. A motion to dismiss based on forum non conveniens shall be served not later than 60 days after service of process on the moving party.

(h) **Retention of Jurisdiction**. The court shall retain jurisdiction after the dismissal to enforce its order of dismissal and any conditions and stipulations in the order.

Rule 1.070 Process

(a) **Summons; Issuance**. Upon the commencement of the action, summons or other process authorized by law shall be issued forthwith by the clerk or judge under the clerk's or the judge's signature and the seal of the court and delivered for service without praecipe.

(b) **Service; By Whom Made**. Service of process may be made by an officer authorized by law to serve process, but the court may appoint any competent person not interested in the action to serve the process. When so appointed, the person serving process shall make proof of service by affidavit promptly and in any event within the time during which the person served must respond to the process. Failure to make proof of service shall not affect the validity of the service. When any process is returned not executed or returned improperly executed for any defendant, the party causing its issuance shall be entitled to such additional process against the unserved party as is required to effect service.

(c) **Service; Numerous Defendants**. If there is more than 1 defendant, the clerk or judge shall issue as many writs of process against the several defendants as may be directed by the plaintiff or the plaintiff's attorney.

(d) **Service by Publication**. Service of process by publication may be made as provided by statute.

(e) **Copies of Initial Pleading for Persons Served**. At the time of personal service of process a copy of the initial pleading shall be delivered to the party upon whom service is made. The date and hour of service shall be endorsed on the original process and all copies of it by the person making the service. The party seeking to effect personal service shall furnish the person making service with the necessary copies. When the service is made by publication, copies of the initial pleadings shall be furnished to the clerk and mailed by the clerk with the notice of action to all parties whose addresses are stated in the initial pleading or sworn statement.

(f) **Service of Orders**. If personal service of a court order is to be made, the original order shall be filed with the clerk, who shall certify or verify a copy of it without charge. The person making service shall use the certified copy instead of the original order in the same manner as original process in making service.

(g) **Fees; Service of Pleadings**. The statutory compensation for making service shall not be increased by the simultaneous delivery or mailing of the copy of the initial pleading in conformity with this rule.

(h) **Pleading Basis**. When service of process is to be made under statutes authorizing service on nonresidents of Florida, it is sufficient to plead the basis for service in the language of the statute without pleading the facts supporting service.

(i) **Service of Process by Mail**. A defendant may accept service of process by mail.

(1) Acceptance of service of a complaint by mail does not thereby waive any objection to the venue or to the jurisdiction of the court over the person of the defendant.

(2) A plaintiff may notify any defendant of the commencement of the action and request that the defendant waive service of a summons. The notice and request shall:

(A) be in writing and be addressed directly to the defendant, if an individual, or to an officer or managing or general agent of the defendant or other agent authorized by appointment or law to receive service of process;

(B) be dispatched by certified mail, return receipt requested;

(C) be accompanied by a copy of the complaint and shall identify the court in which it has been filed;

(D) inform the defendant of the consequences of compliance and of failure to comply with the request;

(E) state the date on which the request is sent;

(F) allow the defendant 20 days from the date on which the request is received to return the waiver, or, if the address of the defendant is outside of the United States, 30 days from the date on which it is received to return the waiver; and

(G) provide the defendant with an extra copy of the notice and request, including the waiver, as well as a prepaid means of compliance in writing.

(3) If a defendant fails to comply with a request for waiver within the time provided herein, the court shall impose the costs subsequently incurred in effecting service on the defendant unless good cause for the failure is shown.

(4) A defendant who, before being served with process, timely returns a waiver so requested is not required to respond to the complaint until 60 days after the date the defendant received the request for waiver of service. For purposes of computing any time prescribed or allowed by these rules, service of process shall be deemed effected 20 days before the time required to respond to the complaint.

(5) When the plaintiff files a waiver of service with the court, the action shall proceed, except as provided in subdivision (4) above, as if a summons and complaint had been served at the time of filing the waiver, and no further proof of service shall be required.

(j) **Summons; Time Limit**. If service of the initial process and initial pleading is not made upon a defendant within 120 days after filing of the initial pleading directed to that defendant the court, on its own initiative after notice or on motion, shall direct that service be effected within a specified time or shall dismiss the action without prejudice or drop that defendant as a party; provided that if the plaintiff shows good cause or excusable neglect for the failure, the court shall extend the time for service for an appropriate period. When a motion for leave to amend with the attached proposed amended complaint is filed, the 120-day period for service of amended complaints on the new party or parties shall begin upon the entry of an order granting leave to amend. A dismissal under this subdivision shall not be considered a voluntary dismissal or operate as an adjudication on the merits under rule 1.420(a)(1).

Rule 1.071 Constitutional Challenge to State Statute or County or Municipal Charter, Ordinance, or Franchise; Notice by Party

A party that files a pleading, written motion, or other paper drawing into question the constitutionality of a state statute or a county or municipal charter, ordinance, or franchise must promptly

(a) file a notice of constitutional question stating the question and identifying the paper that raises it; and

(b) serve the notice and the pleading, written motion, or other paper drawing into question the constitutionality of a state statute or a county or municipal charter, ordinance, or franchise on the

Attorney General or the state attorney of the judicial circuit in which the action is pending, by either certified or registered mail.

Service of the notice and pleading, written motion, or other paper does not require joinder of the Attorney General or the state attorney as a party to the action.

Rule 1.080 Service and Filing of Pleadings, Orders, and Documents

(a) **Service**. Every pleading subsequent to the initial pleading, all orders, and every other document filed or required by statute or rule to be served in the action must be served in conformity with the requirements of Florida Rule of General Practice and Judicial Administration 2.516.

(b) **Filing**. All documents shall be filed in conformity with the requirements of Florida Rule of Judicial Administration 2.525.

(c) **Writing and written defined**. Writing or written means a document containing information, an application, or a stipulation.

Rule 1.090 Time

(a) **Computation**. Computation of time shall be governed by Florida Rule of General Practice and Judicial Administration 2.514.

(b) **Enlargement**.
  (1) *In General*. When an act is required or allowed to be done at or within a specified time by order of court, by these rules, or by notice given thereunder, for cause shown the court at any time in its discretion;
    (A) with or without notice, may order the period enlarged if request therefor is made before the expiration of the period originally prescribed or as extended by a previous order, or
    (B) upon motion made and notice after the expiration of the specified period, may permit the act to be done when failure to act was the result of excusable neglect.
  (2) *Exceptions*. The court may not extend the time for making a motion for new trial, for rehearing, or to alter or amend a judgment; making a motion for relief from a judgment under rule 1.540(b); taking an appeal or filing a petition for certiorari; or making a motion for a directed verdict.

(c) **Unaffected by Expiration of Term**. The period of time provided for the doing of any act or the taking of any proceeding shall not be affected or limited by the continued existence or expiration of a term of court. The continued existence or expiration of a term of court in no way affects the power of a court to do any act or take any proceeding in any action which is or has been pending before it.

(d) **For Motions**. A copy of any written motion which may not be heard ex parte and a copy of the notice of the hearing thereof shall be served a reasonable time before the time specified for the hearing.

Rule 1.100 Pleadings and Motions

(a) **Pleadings**. There shall be a complaint or, when so designated by a statute or rule, a petition, and an answer to it; an answer to a counterclaim denominated as such; an answer to a crossclaim if the answer contains a crossclaim; a third-party complaint if a person who was not an original party is summoned as a third-party defendant; and a third-party answer if a third-party complaint is served. If an answer or third-party answer contains an affirmative defense and the opposing party seeks to avoid it, the opposing party shall file a reply containing the avoidance. No other pleadings shall be allowed.

(b) **Motions**. An application to the court for an order shall be by motion which shall be made in writing unless made during a hearing or trial, shall state with particularity the grounds therefor, and shall set forth the relief or order sought. The requirement of writing is fulfilled if the motion is stated in a written notice of the hearing of the motion. All notices of hearing shall specify each motion or other matter to be heard.

(c) **Caption**.
  (1) Every pleading, motion, order, judgment, or other paper shall have a caption containing the name of the court, the file number, and except for in rem proceedings, including forfeiture proceedings, the name of the first party on each side with an appropriate indication of other parties, and a

designation identifying the party filing it and its nature or the nature of the order, as the case may be. In any in rem proceeding, every pleading, motion, order, judgment, or other paper shall have a caption containing the name of the court, the file number, the style "In re" (followed by the name or general description of the property), and a designation of the person or entity filing it and its nature or the nature of the order, as the case may be. In an in rem forfeiture proceeding, the style shall be "In re forfeiture of" (followed by the name or general description of the property). All papers filed in the action shall be styled in such a manner as to indicate clearly the subject matter of the paper and the party requesting or obtaining relief.

(2) A civil cover sheet (form 1.997) shall be completed and filed with the clerk at the time an initial complaint or petition is filed by the party initiating the action. If the cover sheet is not filed, the clerk shall accept the complaint or petition for filing; but all proceedings in the action shall be abated until a properly executed cover sheet is completed and filed. The clerk shall complete the civil cover sheet for a party appearing pro se.

(3) A final disposition form (form 1.998) shall be filed with the clerk by the prevailing party at the time of the filing of the order or judgment which disposes of the action. If the action is settled without a court order or judgment being entered, or dismissed by the parties, the plaintiff or petitioner immediately shall file a final disposition form (form 1.998) with the clerk. The clerk shall complete the final disposition form for a party appearing pro se, or when the action is dismissed by court order for lack of prosecution pursuant to rule 1.420(e).

(d) **Motion in Lieu of Scire Facias**. Any relief available by scire facias may be granted on motion after notice without the issuance of a writ of scire facias.

Rule 1.110 General Rules of Pleading

(a) **Forms of Pleadings**. Forms of action and technical forms for seeking relief and of pleas, pleadings, or motions are abolished.

(b) **Claims for Relief**. A pleading which sets forth a claim for relief, whether an original claim, counterclaim, crossclaim, or third-party claim, must state a cause of action and shall contain (1) a short and plain statement of the grounds upon which the court's jurisdiction depends, unless the court already has jurisdiction and the claim needs no new grounds of jurisdiction to support it, (2) a short and plain statement of the ultimate facts showing that the pleader is entitled to relief, and (3) a demand for judgment for the relief to which the pleader deems himself or herself entitled. Relief in the alternative or of several different types may be demanded. Every complaint shall be considered to pray for general relief.

(c) **The Answer**. In the answer a pleader shall state in short and plain terms the pleader's defenses to each claim asserted and shall admit or deny the averments on which the adverse party relies. If the defendant is without knowledge, the defendant shall so state and such statement shall operate as a denial. Denial shall fairly meet the substance of the averments denied. When a pleader intends in good faith to deny only a part of an averment, the pleader shall specify so much of it as is true and shall deny the remainder. Unless the pleader intends in good faith to controvert all of the averments of the preceding pleading, the pleader may make denials as specific denials of designated averments or may generally deny all of the averments except such designated averments as the pleader expressly admits, but when the pleader does so intend to controvert all of its averments, including averments of the grounds upon which the court's jurisdiction depends, the pleader may do so by general denial.

(d) **Affirmative Defenses**. In pleading to a preceding pleading a party shall set forth affirmatively accord and satisfaction, arbitration and award, assumption of risk, contributory negligence, discharge in bankruptcy, duress, estoppel, failure of consideration, fraud, illegality, injury by fellow servant, laches, license, payment, release, res judicata, statute of frauds, statute of limitations, waiver, and any other matter constituting an avoidance or affirmative defense. When a party has mistakenly designated a defense as a counterclaim or a counterclaim as a defense, the court, on terms if justice so requires, shall treat the pleading as if there had been a proper designation. Affirmative defenses appearing on the face of a prior pleading may be asserted as grounds for a motion or defense under rule 1.140(b); provided this shall not limit amendments under rule 1.190 even if such ground is sustained.

(e) **Effect of Failure to Deny**. Averments in a pleading to which a responsive pleading is required, other than those as to the amount of damages, are admitted when not denied in the responsive pleading.

Averments in a pleading to which no responsive pleading is required or permitted shall be taken as denied or avoided.

(f) **Separate Statements**. All averments of claim or defense shall be made in consecutively numbered paragraphs, the contents of each of which shall be limited as far as practicable to a statement of a single set of circumstances, and a paragraph may be referred to by number in all subsequent pleadings. Each claim founded upon a separate transaction or occurrence and each defense other than denials shall be stated in a separate count or defense when a separation facilitates the clear presentation of the matter set forth.

(g) **Joinder of Causes of Action; Consistency**. A pleader may set up in the same action as many claims or causes of action or defenses in the same right as the pleader has, and claims for relief may be stated in the alternative if separate items make up the cause of action, or if 2 or more causes of action are joined. A party may also set forth 2 or more statements of a claim or defense alternatively, either in 1 count or defense or in separate counts or defenses. When 2 or more statements are made in the alternative and 1 of them, if made independently, would be sufficient, the pleading is not made insufficient by the insufficiency of 1 or more of the alternative statements. A party may also state as many separate claims or defenses as that party has, regardless of consistency and whether based on legal or equitable grounds or both. All pleadings shall be construed so as to do substantial justice.

(h) **Subsequent Pleadings**. When the nature of an action permits pleadings subsequent to final judgment and the jurisdiction of the court over the parties has not terminated, the initial pleading subsequent to final judgment shall be designated a supplemental complaint or petition. The action shall then proceed in the same manner and time as though the supplemental complaint or petition were the initial pleading in the action, including the issuance of any needed process. This subdivision shall not apply to proceedings that may be initiated by motion under these rules.

Rule 1.115 Pleading Mortgage Foreclosures

(a) **Claim for Relief**. A claim for relief that seeks to foreclose a mortgage or other lien which secures a promissory note on residential real property, including individual units of condominiums and cooperatives designed principally for occupation by one to four families, must: (1) contain affirmative allegations expressly made by the claimant at the time the proceeding is commenced that the claimant is the holder of the original note secured by the mortgage; or (2) allege with specificity the factual basis by which the claimant is a person entitled to enforce the note under section 673.3011, Florida Statutes.

(b) **Delegated Claim for Relief**. If a claimant has been delegated the authority to institute a mortgage foreclosure action on behalf of the person entitled to enforce the note, the claim for relief shall describe the authority of the claimant and identify with specificity the document that grants the claimant the authority to act on behalf of the person entitled to enforce the note. The term "original note" or "original promissory note" means the signed or executed promissory note rather than a copy of it. The term includes any renewal, replacement, consolidation, or amended and restated note or instrument given in renewal, replacement, or substitution for a previous promissory note. The term also includes a transferrable record, as defined by the Uniform Electronic Transaction Act in section 668.50(16), Florida Statutes.

(c) **Possession of Original Promissory Note**. If the claimant is in possession of the original promissory note, the claimant must file under penalty of perjury a certification contemporaneously with the filing of the claim for relief for foreclosure that the claimant is in possession of the original promissory note. The certification must set forth the location of the note, the name and title of the individual giving the certification, the name of the person who personally verified such possession, and the time and date on which the possession was verified. Correct copies of the note and all allonges to the note must be attached to the certification. The original note and the allonges must be filed with the court before the entry of any judgment of foreclosure or judgment on the note.

(d) **Lost, Destroyed, or Stolen Instrument**. If the claimant seeks to enforce a lost, destroyed, or stolen instrument, an affidavit executed under penalty of perjury must be attached to the claim for relief. The affidavit must: (1) detail a clear chain of all endorsements, transfers, or assignments of the promissory note that is the subject of the action; (2) set forth facts showing that the claimant is entitled to enforce a lost, destroyed, or stolen instrument pursuant to section 673.3091, Florida Statutes; and (3) include as exhibits to the affidavit such copies of the note and the allonges to the note, audit reports showing receipt of the original note, or other evidence of the acquisition, ownership, and possession of the note as may be available to the claimant. Adequate protection as required and identified under sections 673.3091(2) and 702.11(1), Florida Statutes, shall be provided before the entry of final judgment.

(e) **Verification**. When filing an action for foreclosure on a mortgage for residential real property the claim for relief shall be verified by the claimant seeking to foreclose the mortgage. When verification of a document is required, the document filed shall include an oath, affirmation, or the following statement: "Under penalties of perjury, I declare that I have read the foregoing, and the facts alleged therein are true and correct to the best of my knowledge and belief."

Rule 1.120 Pleading Special Matters

(a) **Capacity**. It is not necessary to aver the capacity of a party to sue or be sued, the authority of a party to sue or be sued in a representative capacity, or the legal existence of an organized association of persons that is made a party, except to the extent required to show the jurisdiction of the court. The initial pleading served on behalf of a minor party shall specifically aver the age of the minor party. When a party desires to raise an issue as to the legal existence of any party, the capacity of any party to sue or be sued, or the authority of a party to sue or be sued in a representative capacity, that party shall do so by specific negative averment which shall include such supporting particulars as are peculiarly within the pleader's knowledge.

(b) **Fraud, Mistake, Condition of the Mind**. In all averments of fraud or mistake, the circumstances constituting fraud or mistake shall be stated with such particularity as the circumstances may permit. Malice, intent, knowledge, mental attitude, and other condition of mind of a person may be averred generally.

(c) **Conditions Precedent**. In pleading the performance or occurrence of conditions precedent, it is sufficient to aver generally that all conditions precedent have been performed or have occurred. A denial of performance or occurrence shall be made specifically and with particularity.

(d) **Official Document or Act**. In pleading an official document or official act it is sufficient to aver that the document was issued or the act done in compliance with law.

(e) **Judgment or Decree**. In pleading a judgment or decree of a domestic or foreign court, a judicial or quasi-judicial tribunal, or a board or officer, it is sufficient to aver the judgment or decree without setting forth matter showing jurisdiction to render it.

(f) **Time and Place**. For the purpose of testing the sufficiency of a pleading, averments of time and place are material and shall be considered like all other averments of material matter.

(g) **Special Damage**. When items of special damage are claimed, they shall be specifically stated.

Rule 1.130 Attaching Copy of Cause of Action and Exhibits

(a) **Instruments Attached**. All bonds, notes, bills of exchange, contracts, accounts, or documents upon which action may be brought or defense made, or a copy thereof or a copy of the portions thereof material to the pleadings, shall be incorporated in or attached to the pleading. No papers shall be unnecessarily annexed as exhibits. The pleadings shall contain no unnecessary recitals of deeds, documents, contracts, or other instruments.

(b) **Part for All Purposes**. Any exhibit attached to a pleading shall be considered a part thereof for all purposes. Statements in a pleading may be adopted by reference in a different part of the same pleading, in another pleading, or in any motion.

Rule 1.140 Defenses

(a) **When Presented**.

(1) Unless a different time is prescribed in a statute of Florida, a defendant shall serve an answer within 20 days after service of original process and the initial pleading on the defendant, or not later than the date fixed in a notice by publication. A party served with a pleading stating a crossclaim against that party shall serve an answer to it within 20 days after service on that party. The plaintiff shall serve an answer to a counterclaim within 20 days after service of the

counterclaim. If a reply is required, the reply shall be served within 20 days after service of the answer.

(2)

   (A) Except when sued pursuant to section 768.28, Florida Statutes, the state of Florida, an agency of the state, or an officer or employee of the state sued in an official capacity shall serve an answer to the complaint or crossclaim, or a reply to a counterclaim, within 40 days after service.

   (B) When sued pursuant to section 768.28, Florida Statutes, the Department of Financial Services or the defendant state agency shall have 30 days from the date of service within which to serve an answer to the complaint or crossclaim or a reply to a counterclaim.

(3) The service of a motion under this rule, except a motion for judgment on the pleadings or a motion to strike under subdivision (f), alters these periods of time so that if the court denies the motion or postpones its disposition until the trial on the merits, the responsive pleadings shall be served within 10 days after notice of the court's action or, if the court grants a motion for a more definite statement, the responsive pleadings shall be served within 10 days after service of the more definite statement unless a different time is fixed by the court in either case.

(4) If the court permits or requires an amended or responsive pleading or a more definite statement, the pleading or statement shall be served within 10 days after notice of the court's action. Responses to the pleadings or statements shall be served within 10 days of service of the pleadings or statements.

(b) **How Presented**. Every defense in law or fact to a claim for relief in a pleading shall be asserted in the responsive pleading, if one is required, but the following defenses may be made by motion at the option of the pleader: (1) lack of jurisdiction over the subject matter, (2) lack of jurisdiction over the person, (3) improper venue, (4) insufficiency of process, (5) insufficiency of service of process, (6) failure to state a cause of action, and (7) failure to join indispensable parties. A motion making any of these defenses shall be made before pleading if a further pleading is permitted. The grounds on which any of the enumerated defenses are based and the substantial matters of law intended to be argued shall be stated specifically and with particularity in the responsive pleading or motion. Any ground not stated shall be deemed to be waived except any ground showing that the court lacks jurisdiction of the subject matter may be made at any time. No defense or objection is waived by being joined with other defenses or objections in a responsive pleading or motion. If a pleading sets forth a claim for relief to which the adverse party is not required to serve a responsive pleading, the adverse party may assert any defense in law or fact to that claim for relief at the trial, except that the objection of failure to state a legal defense in an answer or reply shall be asserted by motion to strike the defense within 20 days after service of the answer or reply.

(c) **Motion for Judgment on the Pleadings**. After the pleadings are closed, but within such time as not to delay the trial, any party may move for judgment on the pleadings.

(d) **Preliminary Hearings**. The defenses 1 to 7 in subdivision (b) of this rule, whether made in a pleading or by motion, and the motion for judgment in subdivision (c) of this rule shall be heard and determined before trial on application of any party unless the court orders that the hearing and determination shall be deferred until the trial.

(e) **Motion for More Definite Statement**. If a pleading to which a responsive pleading is permitted is so vague or ambiguous that a party cannot reasonably be required to frame a responsive pleading, that party may move for a more definite statement before interposing a responsive pleading. The motion shall point out the defects complained of and the details desired. If the motion is granted and the order of the court is not obeyed within 10 days after notice of the order or such other time as the court may fix, the court may strike the pleading to which the motion was directed or make such order as it deems just.

(f) **Motion to Strike**. A party may move to strike or the court may strike redundant, immaterial, impertinent, or scandalous matter from any pleading at any time.

(g) **Consolidation of Defenses**. A party who makes a motion under this rule may join with it the other motions herein provided for and then available to that party. If a party makes a motion under this rule but omits from it any defenses or objections then available to that party that this rule permits to be raised by motion, that party shall not thereafter make a motion based on any of the defenses or objections omitted, except as provided in subdivision (h)(2) of this rule.

(h) **Waiver of Defenses**.

(1) A party waives all defenses and objections that the party does not present either by motion under subdivisions (b), (e), or (f) of this rule or, if the party has made no motion, in a responsive pleading except as provided in subdivision (h)(2).

(2) The defenses of failure to state a cause of action or a legal defense or to join an indispensable party may be raised by motion for judgment on the pleadings or at the trial on the merits in addition to being raised either in a motion under subdivision (b) or in the answer or reply. The defense of lack of jurisdiction of the subject matter may be raised at any time.

Rule 1.150 Sham Pleadings

(a) **Motion to Strike**. If a party deems any pleading or part thereof filed by another party to be a sham, that party may move to strike the pleading or part thereof before the cause is set for trial and the court shall hear the motion, taking evidence of the respective parties, and if the motion is sustained, the pleading to which the motion is directed shall be stricken. Default and summary judgment on the merits may be entered in the discretion of the court or the court may permit additional pleadings to be filed for good cause shown.

(b) **Contents of Motion**. The motion to strike shall be verified and shall set forth fully the facts on which the movant relies and may be supported by affidavit. No traverse of the motion shall be required.

Rule 1.160 Motions

All motions and applications in the clerk's office for the issuance of mesne process and final process to enforce and execute judgments, for entering defaults, and for such other proceedings in the clerk's office as do not require an order of court shall be deemed motions and applications grantable as of course by the clerk. The clerk's action may be suspended or altered or rescinded by the court upon cause shown.

Rule 1.170 Counterclaims and Crossclaims

(a) **Compulsory Counterclaims**. A pleading shall state as a counterclaim any claim which at the time of serving the pleading the pleader has against any opposing party, provided it arises out of the transaction or occurrence that is the subject matter of the opposing party's claim and does not require for its adjudication the presence of third parties over whom the court cannot acquire jurisdiction. But the pleader need not state a claim if (1) at the time the action was commenced the claim was the subject of another pending action, or (2) the opposing party brought suit upon that party's claim by attachment or other process by which the court did not acquire jurisdiction to render a personal judgment on the claim and the pleader is not stating a counterclaim under this rule.

(b) **Permissive Counterclaim**. A pleading may state as a counterclaim any claim against an opposing party not arising out of the transaction or occurrence that is the subject matter of the opposing party's claim.

(c) **Counterclaim Exceeding Opposing Claim**. A counterclaim may or may not diminish or defeat the recovery sought by the opposing party. It may claim relief exceeding in amount or different in kind from that sought in the pleading of the opposing party.

(d) **Counterclaim against the State**. These rules shall not be construed to enlarge beyond the limits established by law the right to assert counterclaims or to claim credits against the state or any of its subdivisions or other governmental organizations thereof subject to suit or against a municipal corporation or against an officer, agency, or administrative board of the state.

(e) **Counterclaim Maturing or Acquired after Pleading**. A claim which matured or was acquired by the pleader after serving the pleading may be presented as a counterclaim by supplemental pleading with the permission of the court.

(f) **Omitted Counterclaim or Crossclaim**. When a pleader fails to set up a counterclaim or crossclaim through oversight, inadvertence, or excusable neglect, or when justice requires, the pleader may set up the counterclaim or crossclaim by amendment with leave of the court.

(g) **Crossclaim against Co-Party**.

(h) A pleading may state as a crossclaim any claim by one party against a co-party arising out of the transaction or occurrence that is the subject matter of either the original action or a counterclaim therein, or relating to any property that is the subject matter of the original action. The crossclaim may include a claim that the party against whom it is asserted is or may be liable to the crossclaimant for all or part of a claim asserted in the action against the crossclaimant. Service of a crossclaim on a party who has appeared in the action must be made under Florida Rule of General Practice and Judicial Administration. Service of a crossclaim against a party who has not appeared in the action must be made in the manner provided for service of summons.

(i) FL. R. Civ. P. 1.170 Counterclaims and Crossclaims (Florida Rules of Civil Procedure (2022 Edition))

(j) **Additional Parties May Be Brought In**. When the presence of parties other than those to the original action is required to grant complete relief in the determination of a counterclaim or crossclaim, they shall be named in the counterclaim or crossclaim and be served with process and shall be parties to the action thereafter if jurisdiction of them can be obtained and their joinder will not deprive the court of jurisdiction of the action. Rules 1.250(b) and (c) apply to parties brought in under this subdivision.

(k) **Separate Trials; Separate Judgment**. If the court orders separate trials as provided in rule 1.270(b), judgment on a counterclaim or crossclaim may be rendered when the court has jurisdiction to do so even if a claim of the opposing party has been dismissed or otherwise disposed of.

(l) **Demand Exceeding Jurisdiction; Transfer of Action**. If the demand of any counterclaim or crossclaim exceeds the jurisdiction of the court in which the action is pending, the action shall be transferred forthwith to the court of the same county having jurisdiction of the demand in the counterclaim or crossclaim with only such alterations in the pleadings as are essential. The court shall order the transfer of the action and the transmittal of all papers in it to the proper court if the party asserting the demand exceeding the jurisdiction deposits with the court having jurisdiction a sum sufficient to pay the clerk's service charge in the court to which the action is transferred at the time of filing the counterclaim or crossclaim. Thereupon the original papers and deposit shall be transmitted and filed with a certified copy of the order. The court to which the action is transferred shall have full power and jurisdiction over the demands of all parties. Failure to make the service charge deposit at the time the counterclaim or crossclaim is filed, or within such further time as the court may allow, shall reduce a claim for damages to an amount within the jurisdiction of the court where the action is pending and waive the claim in other cases.

Rule 1.180 Third-Party Practice

(a) **When Available**. At any time after commencement of the action a defendant may have a summons and complaint served on a person not a party to the action who is or may be liable to the defendant for all or part of the plaintiff's claim against the defendant, and may also assert any other claim that arises out of the transaction or occurrence that is the subject matter of the plaintiff's claim. The defendant need not obtain leave of court if the defendant files the third-party complaint not later than 20 days after the defendant serves the original answer. Otherwise, the defendant must obtain leave on motion and notice to all parties to the action. The person served with the summons and third-party complaint, herein called the third-party defendant, shall make defenses to the defendant's claim as provided in rules 1.110 and 1.140 and counterclaims against the defendant and crossclaims against other third-party defendants as provided in rule 1.170. The third-party defendant may assert against the plaintiff any defenses that the defendant has to the plaintiff's claim. The third-party defendant may also assert any claim against the plaintiff arising out of the transaction or occurrence that is the subject matter of the plaintiff's claim against the defendant. The plaintiff may assert any claim against the third-party defendant arising out of the transaction or occurrence that is the subject matter of the plaintiff's claim against the defendant, and the third-party defendant thereupon shall assert a defense as provided in rules 1.110 and 1.140 and counterclaims and crossclaims as provided in rule 1.170. Any party may move to strike the third-party claim or for its severance or separate trial. A third-party defendant may proceed under this rule against any person not a party to the action who is or may be liable to the third-party defendant for all or part of the claim made in the action against the third-party defendant.

(b) **When Plaintiff May Bring in Third Party**. When a counterclaim is asserted against the plaintiff, the plaintiff may bring in a third party under circumstances which would entitle a defendant to do so under this rule.

Rule 1.190 Amended and Supplemental Pleadings

(a) **Amendments**. A party may amend a pleading once as a matter of course at any time before a responsive pleading is served or, if the pleading is one to which no responsive pleading is permitted and the action has not been placed on the trial calendar, may so amend it at any time within 20 days after it is served. Otherwise a party may amend a pleading only by leave of court or by written consent of the adverse party. If a party files a motion to amend a pleading, the party shall attach the proposed amended pleading to the motion. Leave of court shall be given freely when justice so requires. A party shall plead in response to an amended pleading within 10 days after service of the amended pleading unless the court otherwise orders.

(b) **Amendments to Conform with the Evidence**. When issues not raised by the pleadings are tried by express or implied consent of the parties, they shall be treated in all respects as if they had been raised in the pleadings. Such amendment of the pleadings as may be necessary to cause them to conform to the evidence and to raise these issues may be made upon motion of any party at any time, even after judgment, but failure so to amend shall not affect the result of the trial of these issues. If the evidence is objected to at the trial on the ground that it is not within the issues made by the pleadings, the court may allow the pleadings to be amended to conform with the evidence and shall do so freely when the merits of the cause are more effectually presented thereby and the objecting party fails to satisfy the court that the admission of such evidence will prejudice the objecting party in maintaining an action or defense upon the merits.

(c) **Relation Back of Amendments**. When the claim or defense asserted in the amended pleading arose out of the conduct, transaction, or occurrence set forth or attempted to be set forth in the original pleading, the amendment shall relate back to the date of the original pleading.

(d) **Supplemental Pleadings**. Upon motion of a party the court may permit that party, upon reasonable notice and upon such terms as are just, to serve a supplemental pleading setting forth transactions or occurrences or events which have happened since the date of the pleading sought to be supplemented. If the court deems it advisable that the adverse party plead thereto, it shall so order, specifying the time therefor.

(e) **Amendments Generally**. At any time in furtherance of justice, upon such terms as may be just, the court may permit any process, proceeding, pleading, or record to be amended or material supplemental matter to be set forth in an amended or supplemental pleading. At every stage of the action the court must disregard any error or defect in the proceedings which does not affect the substantial rights of the parties.

(f) **Claims for Punitive Damages**. A motion for leave to amend a pleading to assert a claim for punitive damages shall make a reasonable showing, by evidence in the record or evidence to be proffered by the claimant, that provides a reasonable basis for recovery of such damages. The motion to amend can be filed separately and before the supporting evidence or proffer, but each shall be served on all parties at least 20 days before the hearing.

Rule 1.200 Pretrial Procedure

(a) **Case Management Conference**. At any time after responsive pleadings or motions are due, the court may order, or a party, by serving a notice, may convene, a case management conference. The matter to be considered shall be specified in the order or notice setting the conference. At such a conference the court may:

  (1) schedule or reschedule the service of motions, pleadings, and other papers;

  (2) set or reset the time of trials, subject to rule 1.440(c);

  (3) coordinate the progress of the action if the complex litigation factors contained in rule 1.201(a)(2)(A)-(a)(2)(H) are present;

  (4) limit, schedule, order, or expedite discovery;

  (5) consider the possibility of obtaining admissions of fact and voluntary exchange of documents and electronically stored information, and stipulations regarding authenticity of documents and electronically stored information;

  (6) consider the need for advance rulings from the court on the admissibility of documents and electronically stored information;

(7) discuss as to electronically stored information, the possibility of agreements from the parties regarding the extent to which such evidence should be preserved, the form in which such evidence should be produced, and whether discovery of such information should be conducted in phases or limited to particular individuals, time periods, or sources;

(8) schedule disclosure of expert witnesses and the discovery of facts known and opinions held by such experts;

(9) schedule or hear motions in limine;

(10) pursue the possibilities of settlement;

(11) require filing of preliminary stipulations if issues can be narrowed;

(12) consider referring issues to a magistrate for findings of fact; and

(13) schedule other conferences or determine other matters that may aid in the disposition of the action.

(b) **Pretrial Conference**. After the action is at issue the court itself may or shall on the timely motion of any party require the parties to appear for a conference to consider and determine:

(1) the simplification of the issues;

(2) the necessity or desirability of amendments to the pleadings;

(3) the possibility of obtaining admissions of fact and of documents that will avoid unnecessary proof;

(4) the limitation of the number of expert witnesses;

(5) the potential use of juror notebooks; and

(6) any matters permitted under subdivision (a) of this rule.

(c) **Notice**. Reasonable notice shall be given for a case management conference, and 20 days' notice shall be given for a pretrial conference. On failure of a party to attend a conference, the court may dismiss the action, strike the pleadings, limit proof or witnesses, or take any other appropriate action. Any documents that the court requires for any conference shall be specified in the order. Orders setting pretrial conferences shall be uniform throughout the territorial jurisdiction of the court.

(d) **Pretrial Order**. The court shall make an order reciting the action taken at a conference and any stipulations made. The order shall control the subsequent course of the action unless modified to prevent injustice.

Rule 1.201 Complex Litigation

(a) **Complex Litigation Defined**. At any time after all defendants have been served, and an appearance has been entered in response to the complaint by each party or a default entered, any party, or the court on its own motion, may move to declare an action complex. However, any party may move to designate an action complex before all defendants have been served subject to a showing to the court why service has not been made on all defendants. The court shall convene a hearing to determine whether the action requires the use of complex litigation procedures and enter an order within 10 days of the conclusion of the hearing.

(1) A "complex action" is one that is likely to involve complicated legal or case management issues and that may require extensive judicial management to expedite the action, keep costs reasonable, or promote judicial efficiency.

(2) In deciding whether an action is complex, the court must consider whether the action is likely to involve:

(A) numerous pretrial motions raising difficult or novel legal issues or legal issues that are inextricably intertwined that will be time-consuming to resolve;

(B) management of a large number of separately represented parties;

(C) coordination with related actions pending in one or more courts in other counties, states, or countries, or in a federal court;

(D) pretrial management of a large number of witnesses or a substantial amount of documentary evidence;

(E) substantial time required to complete the trial;

(F) management at trial of a large number of experts, witnesses, attorneys, or exhibits;

(G) substantial post-judgment judicial supervision; and

(H) any other analytical factors identified by the court or a party that tend to complicate comparable actions and which are likely to arise in the context of the instant action.

(3)   If all of the parties, pro se or through counsel, sign and file with the clerk of the court a written stipulation to the fact that an action is complex and identifying the factors in (2)(A) through (2)(H) above that apply, the court shall enter an order designating the action as complex without a hearing.

(b)   **Initial Case Management Report and Conference**. The court shall hold an initial case management conference within 60 days from the date of the order declaring the action complex.

(1)   At least 20 days prior to the date of the initial case management conference, attorneys for the parties as well as any parties appearing pro se shall confer and prepare a joint statement, which shall be filed with the clerk of the court no later than 14 days before the conference, outlining a discovery plan and stating:

(A)   a brief factual statement of the action, which includes the claims and defenses;

(B)   a brief statement on the theory of damages by any party seeking affirmative relief;

(C)   the likelihood of settlement;

(D)   the likelihood of appearance in the action of additional parties and identification of any nonparties to whom any of the parties will seek to allocate fault;

(E)   the proposed limits on the time: (i) to join other parties and to amend the pleadings, (ii) to file and hear motions, (iii) to identify any nonparties whose identity is known, or otherwise describe as specifically as practicable any nonparties whose identity is not known, (iv) to disclose expert witnesses, and (v) to complete discovery;

(F)   the names of the attorneys responsible for handling the action;

(G)   the necessity for a protective order to facilitate discovery;

(H)   proposals for the formulation and simplification of issues, including the elimination of frivolous claims or defenses, and the number and timing of motions for summary judgment or partial summary judgment;

(I)   the possibility of obtaining admissions of fact and voluntary exchange of documents and electronically stored information, stipulations regarding authenticity of documents, electronically stored information, and the need for advance rulings from the court on admissibility of evidence;

(J)   the possibility of obtaining agreements among the parties regarding the extent to which such electronically stored information should be preserved, the form in which such information should be produced, and whether discovery of such information should be conducted in phases or limited to particular individuals, time periods, or sources;

(K)   suggestions on the advisability and timing of referring matters to a magistrate, master, other neutral, or mediation;

(L)   a preliminary estimate of the time required for trial;

(M)   requested date or dates for conferences before trial, a final pretrial conference, and trial;

(N)   a description of pertinent documents and a list of fact witnesses the parties believe to be relevant;

(O)   number of experts and fields of expertise; and

(P)   any other information that might be helpful to the court in setting further conferences and the trial date.

(2)   Lead trial counsel and a client representative shall attend the initial case management conference.

(3)   Notwithstanding rule 1.440, at the initial case management conference, the court will set the trial date or dates no sooner than 6 months and no later than 24 months from the date of the conference unless good cause is shown for an earlier or later setting. The trial date or dates shall be on a docket having sufficient time within which to try the action and, when feasible, for a date or dates certain. The trial date shall be set after consultation with counsel and in the presence of all clients or authorized client representatives. The court shall, no later than 2 months prior to the date scheduled for jury selection, arrange for a sufficient number of available jurors. Continuance of the trial of a complex action should rarely be granted and then only upon good cause shown.

(c)   **The Case Management Order**. The case management order shall address each matter set forth under rule 1.200(a) and set the action for a pretrial conference and trial. The case management order also shall specify the following:

(1)   Dates by which all parties shall name their expert witnesses and provide the expert information required by rule 1.280(b)(5). If a party has named an expert witness in a field in which any other

parties have not identified experts, the other parties may name experts in that field within 30 days thereafter. No additional experts may be named unless good cause is shown.

(2) Not more than 10 days after the date set for naming experts, the parties shall meet and schedule dates for deposition of experts and all other witnesses not yet deposed. At the time of the meeting each party is responsible for having secured three confirmed dates for its expert witnesses. In the event the parties cannot agree on a discovery deposition schedule, the court, upon motion, shall set the schedule. Any party may file the completed discovery deposition schedule agreed upon or entered by the court. Once filed, the deposition dates in the schedule shall not be altered without consent of all parties or upon order of the court. Failure to comply with the discovery schedule may result in sanctions in accordance with rule 1.380.

(3) Dates by which all parties are to complete all other discovery.

(4) The court shall schedule periodic case management conferences and hearings on lengthy motions at reasonable intervals based on the particular needs of the action. The attorneys for the parties as well as any parties appearing pro se shall confer no later than 15 days prior to each case management conference or hearing. They shall notify the court at least 10 days prior to any case management conference or hearing if the parties stipulate that a case management conference or hearing time is unnecessary. Failure to timely notify the court that a case management conference or hearing time is unnecessary may result in sanctions.

(5) The case management order may include a briefing schedule setting forth a time period within which to file briefs or memoranda, responses, and reply briefs or memoranda, prior to the court considering such matters.

(6) A deadline for conducting alternative dispute resolution.

(d) **Final Case Management Conference**. The court shall schedule a final case management conference not less than 90 days prior to the date the case is set for trial. At least 10 days prior to the final case management conference the parties shall confer to prepare a case status report, which shall be filed with the clerk of the court either prior to or at the time of the final case management conference. The status report shall contain in separately numbered paragraphs:

(1) A list of all pending motions requiring action by the court and the date those motions are set for hearing.

(2) Any change regarding the estimated trial time.

(3) The names of the attorneys who will try the case.

(4) A list of the names and addresses of all non-expert witnesses (including impeachment and rebuttal witnesses) intended to be called at trial. However, impeachment or rebuttal witnesses not identified in the case status report may be allowed to testify if the need for their testimony could not have been reasonably foreseen at the time the case status report was prepared.

(5) A list of all exhibits intended to be offered at trial.

(6) Certification that copies of witness and exhibit lists will be filed with the clerk of the court at least 48 hours prior to the date and time of the final case management conference.

(7) A deadline for the filing of amended lists of witnesses and exhibits, which amendments shall be allowed only upon motion and for good cause shown.

(8) Any other matters which could impact the timely and effective trial of the action.

Rule 1.210 Parties

(a) **Parties Generally**. Every action may be prosecuted in the name of the real party in interest, but a personal representative, administrator, guardian, trustee of an express trust, a party with whom or in whose name a contract has been made for the benefit of another, or a party expressly authorized by statute may sue in that person's own name without joining the party for whose benefit the action is brought. All persons having an interest in the subject of the action and in obtaining the relief demanded may join as plaintiffs and any person may be made a defendant who has or claims an interest adverse to the plaintiff. Any person may at any time be made a party if that person's presence is necessary or proper to a complete determination of the cause. Persons having a united interest may be joined on the same side as plaintiffs or defendants, and anyone who refuses to join may for such reason be made a defendant.

(b) **Minors or Incompetent Persons**. When a minor or incompetent person has a representative, such as a guardian or other like fiduciary, the representative may sue or defend on behalf of the minor or incompetent person. A minor or incompetent person who does not have a duly appointed representative may sue by next friend or by a guardian ad litem. The court shall appoint a guardian ad litem for a minor or incompetent person not otherwise represented in an action or shall make such other order as it deems proper for the protection of the minor or incompetent person.

Rule 1.220 Class Actions

(a) **Prerequisites to Class Representation**. Before any claim or defense may be maintained on behalf of a class by one party or more suing or being sued as the representative of all the members of a class, the court shall first conclude that (1) the members of the class are so numerous that separate joinder of each member is impracticable, (2) the claim or defense of the representative party raises questions of law or fact common to the questions of law or fact raised by the claim or defense of each member of the class, (3) the claim or defense of the representative party is typical of the claim or defense of each member of the class, and (4) the representative party can fairly and adequately protect and represent the interests of each member of the class.

(b) **Claims and Defenses Maintainable**. A claim or defense may be maintained on behalf of a class if the court concludes that the prerequisites of subdivision (a) are satisfied, and that:
  (1) the prosecution of separate claims or defenses by or against individual members of the class would create a risk of either:
    (A) inconsistent or varying adjudications concerning individual members of the class which would establish incompatible standards of conduct for the party opposing the class; or
    (B) adjudications concerning individual members of the class which would, as a practical matter, be dispositive of the interests of other members of the class who are not parties to the adjudications, or substantially impair or impede the ability of other members of the class who are not parties to the adjudications to protect their interests; or
  (2) the party opposing the class has acted or refused to act on grounds generally applicable to all the members of the class, thereby making final injunctive relief or declaratory relief concerning the class as a whole appropriate; or
  (3) the claim or defense is not maintainable under either subdivision (b)(1) or (b)(2), but the questions of law or fact common to the claim or defense of the representative party and the claim or defense of each member of the class predominate over any question of law or fact affecting only individual members of the class, and class representation is superior to other available methods for the fair and efficient adjudication of the controversy. The conclusions shall be derived from consideration of all relevant facts and circumstances, including (A) the respective interests of each member of the class in individually controlling the prosecution of separate claims or defenses, (B) the nature and extent of any pending litigation to which any member of the class is a party and in which any question of law or fact controverted in the subject action is to be adjudicated, (C) the desirability or undesirability of concentrating the litigation in the forum where the subject action is instituted, and (D) the difficulties likely to be encountered in the management of the claim or defense on behalf of a class.

(c) **Pleading Requirements**. Any pleading, counterclaim, or crossclaim alleging the existence of a class shall contain the following:
  (1) Next to its caption the designation: "Class Representation."
  (2) Under a separate heading, designated as "Class Representation Allegations," specific recitation of:
    (A) the particular provision of subdivision (b) under which it is claimed that the claim or defense is maintainable on behalf of a class;
    (B) the questions of law or fact that are common to the claim or defense of the representative party and the claim or defense of each member of the class;
    (C) the particular facts and circumstances that show the claim or defense advanced by the representative party is typical of the claim or defense of each member of the class;
    (D) (i) the approximate number of class members, (ii) a definition of the alleged class, and (iii) the particular facts and circumstances that show the representative party will fairly and adequately protect and represent the interests of each member of the class; and

(E) the particular facts and circumstances that support the conclusions required of the court in determining that the action may be maintained as a class action pursuant to the particular provision of subdivision (b) under which it is claimed that the claim or defense is maintainable on behalf of a class.

(d) **Determination of Class Representation; Notice; Judgment: Claim or Defense Maintained Partly on Behalf of a Class**.

    (1) As soon as practicable after service of any pleading alleging the existence of a class under this rule and before service of an order for pretrial conference or a notice for trial, after hearing the court shall enter an order determining whether the claim or defense is maintainable on behalf of a class on the application of any party or on the court's initiative. Irrespective of whether the court determines that the claim or defense is maintainable on behalf of a class, the order shall separately state the findings of fact and conclusions of law upon which the determination is based. In making the determination the court (A) may allow the claim or defense to be so maintained, and, if so, shall state under which subsection of subdivision (b) the claim or defense is to be maintained, (B) may disallow the class representation and strike the class representation allegations, or (C) may order postponement of the determination pending the completion of discovery concerning whether the claim or defense is maintainable on behalf of a class. If the court rules that the claim or defense shall be maintained on behalf of a class under subdivision (b)(3), the order shall also provide for the notice required by subdivision (d)(2). If the court rules that the claim or defense shall be maintained on behalf of a class under subdivision (b)(1) or subdivision (b)(2), the order shall also provide for the notice required by subdivision (d)(2), except when a showing is made that the notice is not required, the court may provide for another kind of notice to the class as is appropriate. When the court orders postponement of its determination, the court shall also establish a date, if possible, for further consideration and final disposition of the motion. An order under this subsection may be conditional and may be altered or amended before entry of a judgment on the merits of the action.

    (2) As soon as is practicable after the court determines that a claim or defense is maintainable on behalf of a class, notice of the pendency of the claim or defense shall be given by the party asserting the existence of the class to all the members of the class. The notice shall be given to each member of the class who can be identified and located through reasonable effort and shall be given to the other members of the class in the manner determined by the court to be most practicable under the circumstances. Unless otherwise ordered by the court, the party asserting the existence of the class shall initially pay for the cost of giving notice. The notice shall inform each member of the class that (A) any member of the class who files a statement with the court by the date specified in the notice asking to be excluded shall be excluded from the class, (B) the judgment, whether favorable or not, will include all members who do not request exclusion, and (C) any member who does not request exclusion may make a separate appearance within the time specified in the notice.

    (3) The judgment determining a claim or defense maintained on behalf of a class under subdivision (b)(1) or (b)(2), whether or not favorable to the class, shall include and describe those persons whom the court finds to be members of the class. The judgment determining a claim or defense maintained on behalf of a class under subdivision (b)(3), whether or not favorable to the class, shall include and identify those to whom the notice provided in subdivision (d)(2) was directed, who have not requested exclusion and whom the court finds to be members of the class.

    (4) When appropriate, (A) a claim or defense may be brought or maintained on behalf of a class concerning particular issues, or (B) class representation may be divided into subclasses, and each subclass may be treated as a separate and distinct class and the provisions of this rule shall be applied accordingly.

(e) **Dismissal or Compromise**. After a claim or defense is determined to be maintainable on behalf of a class under subdivision (d), the claim or defense shall not be voluntarily withdrawn, dismissed, or compromised without approval of the court after notice and hearing. Notice of any proposed voluntary withdrawal, dismissal, or compromise shall be given to all members of the class as the court directs.

Rule 1.221 Homeowners' Associations and Condominium Associations

A homeowners' or condominium association, after control of such association is obtained by homeowners or unit owners other than the developer, may institute, maintain, settle, or appeal actions or hearings in its name on behalf of all association members concerning matters of common interest to the members, including, but not limited to: (1) the common property, area, or elements; (2) the roof or structural components of a building, or other improvements (in the case of homeowners' associations, being specifically limited to those improvements for which the association is responsible); (3) mechanical, electrical, or plumbing elements serving a property or an improvement or building (in the case of homeowners' associations, being specifically limited to those elements for which the association is responsible); (4) representations of the developer pertaining to any existing or proposed commonly used facility; (5) protests of ad valorem taxes on commonly used facilities; and, in the case of homeowners' associations, (6) defense of actions in eminent domain or prosecution of inverse condemnation actions. If an association has the authority to maintain a class action under this rule, the association may be joined in an action as representative of that class with reference to litigation and disputes involving the matters for which the association could bring a class action under this rule. Nothing herein limits any statutory or common law right of any individual homeowner or unit owner, or class of such owners, to bring any action that may otherwise be available. An action under this rule shall not be subject to the requirements of rule 1.220.

Rule 1.222 Mobile Homeowners' Associations

A mobile homeowners' association may institute, maintain, settle, or appeal actions or hearings in its name on behalf of all homeowners concerning matters of common interest, including, but not limited to: the common property; structural components of a building or other improvements; mechanical, electrical, and plumbing elements serving the park property; and protests of ad valorem taxes on commonly used facilities. If the association has the authority to maintain a class action under this rule, the association may be joined in an action as representative of that class with reference to litigation and disputes involving the matters for which the association could bring a class action under this rule. Nothing herein limits any statutory or common law right of any individual homeowner or class of homeowners to bring any action which may otherwise be available. An action under this rule shall not be subject to the requirements of rule 1.220.

Rule 1.230 Interventions

Anyone claiming an interest in pending litigation may at any time be permitted to assert a right by intervention, but the intervention shall be in subordination to, and in recognition of, the propriety of the main proceeding, unless otherwise ordered by the court in its discretion.

Rule 1.240 Interpleader

Persons having claims against the plaintiff may be joined as defendants and required to interplead when their claims are such that the plaintiff is or may be exposed to double or multiple liability. It is not ground for objection to the joinder that the claim of the several claimants or the titles on which their claims depend do not have a common origin or are not identical but are adverse to and independent of one another, or that the plaintiff avers that the plaintiff is not liable in whole or in part to any or all of the claimants. A defendant exposed to similar liability may obtain such interpleader by way of crossclaim or counterclaim. The provisions of this rule supplement and do not in any way limit the joinder of parties otherwise permitted.

Rule 1.250 Misjoinder and Nonjoinder f Parties

(a) **Misjoinder**. Misjoinder of parties is not a ground for dismissal of an action. Any claim against a party may be severed and proceeded with separately.
(b) **Dropping Parties**. Parties may be dropped by an adverse party in the manner provided for voluntary dismissal in rule 1.420(a)(1) subject to the exception stated in that rule. If notice of lis pendens has been filed in the action against a party so dropped, the notice of dismissal shall be recorded and cancels the notice of lis pendens without the necessity of a court order. Parties may be dropped by order of court on its own initiative or the motion of any party at any stage of the action on such terms as are just.

(c) **Adding Parties**. Parties may be added once as a matter of course within the same time that pleadings can be so amended under rule 1.190(a). If amendment by leave of court or stipulation of the parties is permitted, parties may be added in the amended pleading without further order of court. Parties may be added by order of court on its own initiative or on motion of any party at any stage of the action and on such terms as are just.

Rule 1.260 Survivor; Substitution of Parties

(a) **Death**.
   (1) If a party dies and the claim is not thereby extinguished, the court may order substitution of the proper parties. The motion for substitution may be made by any party or by the successors or representatives of the deceased party and, together with the notice of hearing, shall be filed and served on all parties as provided in Florida Rule of General Practice and Judicial Administration 2.516 and upon persons not parties in the manner provided for the service of a summons. Unless the motion for substitution is made within 90 days after noting the death is filed and served on all parties as provided in Rule of General Practice and Judicial Administration 2.516, the action shall be dismissed as to the deceased party.
   (2) In the event of the death of one or more of the plaintiffs or of one or more of the defendants in an action in which the right sought to be enforced survives only to the surviving plaintiffs or only against the surviving defendants, the action shall not abate. A statement noting the death shall be filed and served on all parties as provided in Rule of General Practice and Judicial Administration 2.516 and the action shall proceed in favor of or against the surviving parties.

(b) **Incompetency**. If a party becomes incompetent, the court, upon motion filed and served as provided in subdivision (a) of this rule, may allow the action to be continued by or against that person's representative.

(c) **Transfer of Interest**. In case of any transfer of interest, the action may be continued by or against the original party, unless the court upon motion directs the person to whom the interest is transferred to be substituted in the action or joined with the original party. Service of the motion shall be made as provided in subdivision (a) of this rule.

(d) **Public Officers; Death or Separation from Office**.
   (1) When a public officer is a party to an action in an official capacity and during its pendency dies, resigns, or otherwise ceases to hold office, the action does not abate and the officer's successor is automatically substituted as a party. Proceedings following the substitution shall be in the name of the substituted party, but any misnomer not affecting the substantial rights of the parties shall be disregarded. An order of substitution may be entered at any time, but the omission to enter such an order shall not affect the substitution.
   (2) When a public officer sues or is sued in an official capacity, the officer may be described as a party by the official title rather than by name but the court may require the officer's name to be added.

Rule 1.270 Consolidation; Separate Trials

(a) **Consolidation**. When actions involving a common question of law or fact are pending before the court, it may order a joint hearing or trial of any or all the matters in issue in the actions; it may order all the actions consolidated; and it may make such orders concerning proceedings therein as may tend to avoid unnecessary costs or delay.

(b) **Separate Trials**. The court in furtherance of convenience or to avoid prejudice may order a separate trial of any claim, crossclaim, counterclaim, or third-party claim or of any separate issue or of any number of claims, crossclaims, counterclaims, third-party claims, or issues.

Rule 1.280 General Provisions Governing Discovery

(a) **Discovery Methods**. Parties may obtain discovery by one or more of the following methods: depositions upon oral examination or written questions; written interrogatories; production of documents or things or permission to enter upon land or other property for inspection and other purposes; physical and mental examinations; and requests for admission. Unless the court orders otherwise and under subdivision (c) of this rule, the frequency of use of these methods is not limited, except as provided in rules 1.200, 1.340, and 1.370.

(b) **Scope of Discovery**. Unless otherwise limited by order of the court in accordance with these rules, the scope of discovery is as follows:

(1) *In General*. Parties may obtain discovery regarding any matter, not privileged, that is relevant to the subject matter of the pending action, whether it relates to the claim or defense of the party seeking discovery or the claim or defense of any other party, including the existence, description, nature, custody, condition, and location of any books, documents, or other tangible things and the identity and location of persons having knowledge of any discoverable matter. It is not ground for objection that the information sought will be inadmissible at the trial if the information sought appears reasonably calculated to lead to the discovery of admissible evidence.

(2) *Indemnity Agreements*. A party may obtain discovery of the existence and contents of any agreement under which any person may be liable to satisfy part or all of a judgment that may be entered in the action or to indemnify or to reimburse a party for payments made to satisfy the judgment. Information concerning the agreement is not admissible in evidence at trial by reason of disclosure.

(3) *Electronically Stored Information*. A party may obtain discovery of electronically stored information in accordance with these rules.

(4) *Trial Preparation: Materials*. Subject to the provisions of subdivision (b)(5) of this rule, a party may obtain discovery of documents and tangible things otherwise discoverable under subdivision (b)(1) of this rule and prepared in anticipation of litigation or for trial by or for another party or by or for that party's representative, including that party's attorney, consultant, surety, indemnitor, insurer, or agent, only upon a showing that the party seeking discovery has need of the materials in the preparation of the case and is unable without undue hardship to obtain the substantial equivalent of the materials by other means. In ordering discovery of the materials when the required showing has been made, the court shall protect against disclosure of the mental impressions, conclusions, opinions, or legal theories of an attorney or other representative of a party concerning the litigation. Without the required showing a party may obtain a copy of a statement concerning the action or its subject matter previously made by that party. Upon request without the required showing a person not a party may obtain a copy of a statement concerning the action or its subject matter previously made by that person. If the request is refused, the person may move for an order to obtain a copy. The provisions of rule 1.380(a)(4) apply to the award of expenses incurred as a result of making the motion. For purposes of this paragraph, a statement previously made is a written statement signed or otherwise adopted or approved by the person making it, or a stenographic, mechanical, electrical, or other recording or transcription of it that is a substantially verbatim recital of an oral statement by the person making it and contemporaneously recorded.

(5) *Trial Preparation: Experts*. Discovery of facts known and opinions held by experts, otherwise discoverable under the provisions of subdivision (b)(1) of this rule and acquired or developed in anticipation of litigation or for trial, may be obtained only as follows:

(A)

    (i) By interrogatories a party may require any other party to identify each person whom the other party expects to call as an expert witness at trial and to state the subject matter on which the expert is expected to testify, and to state the substance of the facts and opinions to which the expert is expected to testify and a summary of the grounds for each opinion.

    (ii) Any person disclosed by interrogatories or otherwise as a person expected to be called as an expert witness at trial may be deposed in accordance with rule 1.390 without motion or order of court.

    (iii) A party may obtain the following discovery regarding any person disclosed by interrogatories or otherwise as a person expected to be called as an expert witness at trial:

        1. The scope of employment in the pending case and the compensation for such service.

        2. The expert's general litigation experience, including the percentage of work performed for plaintiffs and defendants.

　　　　3.　The identity of other cases, within a reasonable time period, in which the expert has testified by deposition or at trial.

　　　　4.　An approximation of the portion of the expert's involvement as an expert witness, which may be based on the number of hours, percentage of hours, or percentage of earned income derived from serving as an expert witness; however, the expert shall not be required to disclose his or her earnings as an expert witness or income derived from other services.

　　　An expert may be required to produce financial and business records only under the most un-usual or compelling circumstances and may not be compelled to compile or produce nonexistent documents. Upon motion, the court may order further discovery by other means, subject to such restrictions as to scope and other provisions pursuant to subdivision (b)(5)(C) of this rule concerning fees and expenses as the court may deem appropriate.

　(B)　A party may discover facts known or opinions held by an expert who has been retained or specially employed by another party in anticipation of litigation or preparation for trial and who is not expected to be called as a witness at trial, only as provided in rule 1.360(b) or upon a showing of exceptional circumstances under which it is impracticable for the party seeking discovery to obtain facts or opinions on the same subject by other means.

　(C)　Unless manifest injustice would result, the court shall require that the party seeking discovery pay the expert a reasonable fee for time spent in responding to discovery under subdivisions (b)(5)(A) and (b)(5)(B) of this rule; and concerning discovery from an expert obtained under subdivision (b)(5)(A) of this rule the court may require, and concerning discovery obtained under subdivision (b)(5)(B) of this rule shall require, the party seeking discovery to pay the other party a fair part of the fees and expenses reasonably incurred by the latter party in obtaining facts and opinions from the expert.

　(D)　As used in these rules an expert shall be an expert witness as defined in rule 1.390(a).

　(6)　*Claims of Privilege or Protection of Trial Preparation Materials.* When a party withholds information otherwise discoverable under these rules by claiming that it is privileged or subject to protection as trial preparation material, the party shall make the claim expressly and shall describe the nature of the documents, communications, or things not produced or disclosed in a manner that, without revealing information itself privileged or protected, will enable other parties to assess the applicability of the privilege or protection.

(c)　**Protective Orders**. Upon motion by a party or by the person from whom discovery is sought, and for good cause shown, the court in which the action is pending may make any order to protect a party or person from annoyance, embarrassment, oppression, or undue burden or expense that justice requires, including one or more of the following:

　(1)　that the discovery not be had;

　(2)　that the discovery may be had only on specified terms and conditions, including a designation of the time or place;

　(3)　that the discovery may be had only by a method of discovery other than that selected by the party seeking discovery;

　(4)　that certain matters not be inquired into, or that the scope of the discovery be limited to certain matters;

　(5)　that discovery be conducted with no one present except persons designated by the court;

　(6)　that a deposition after being sealed be opened only by order of the court;

　(7)　that a trade secret or other confidential research, development, or commercial information not be disclosed or be disclosed only in a designated way; and

　(8)　that the parties simultaneously file specified documents or information enclosed in sealed envelopes to be opened as directed by the court. If the motion for a protective order is denied in whole or in part, the court may, on such terms and conditions as are just, order that any party or person provide or permit discovery. The provisions of rule 1.380(a)(4) apply to the award of expenses incurred in relation to the motion.

(d)　**Limitations on Discovery of Electronically Stored Information**.

　(1)　A person may object to discovery of electronically stored information from sources that the person identifies as not reasonably accessible because of burden or cost. On motion to compel discovery or for a protective order, the person from whom discovery is sought must show that the information sought or the format requested is not reasonably accessible because of undue burden or cost. If that showing is made, the court may nonetheless order the discovery from such sources or in such formats if the requesting party shows good cause. The court may specify conditions of the discovery, including ordering that some or all of the expenses incurred by the person from whom discovery is sought be paid by the party seeking the discovery.

(2) In determining any motion involving discovery of electronically stored information, the court must limit the frequency or extent of discovery otherwise allowed by these rules if it determines that (i) the discovery sought is unreasonably cumulative or duplicative, or can be obtained from another source or in another manner that is more convenient, less burdensome, or less expensive; or (ii) the burden or expense of the discovery outweighs its likely benefit, considering the needs of the case, the amount in controversy, the parties' resources, the importance of the issues at stake in the action, and the importance of the discovery in resolving the issues.

(e) **Sequence and Timing of Discovery**. Except as provided in subdivision (b)(5) or unless the court upon motion for the convenience of parties and witnesses and in the interest of justice orders otherwise, methods of discovery may be used in any sequence, and the fact that a party is conducting discovery, whether by deposition or otherwise, shall not delay any other party's discovery.

(f) **Supplementing of Responses**. A party who has responded to a request for discovery with a response that was complete when made is under no duty to supplement the response to include information thereafter acquired.

(g) **Court Filing of Documents and Discovery**. Information obtained during discovery shall not be filed with the court until such time as it is filed for good cause. The requirement of good cause is satisfied only where the filing of the information is allowed or required by another applicable rule of procedure or by court order. All filings of discovery documents shall comply with Florida Rule of Judicial Administration 2.425. The court shall have authority to impose sanctions for violation of this rule.

(h) **Apex Doctrine**. A current or former high-level government or corporate officer may seek an order preventing the officer from being subject to a deposition. The motion, whether by a party or by the person of whom the deposition is sought, must be accompanied by an affidavit or declaration of the officer explaining that the officer lacks unique, personal knowledge of the issues being litigated. If the officer meets this burden of production, the court shall issue an order preventing the deposition, unless the party seeking the deposition demonstrates that it has exhausted other discovery, that such discovery is inadequate, and that the officer has unique, personal knowledge of discoverable information. The court may vacate or modify the order if, after additional discovery, the party seeking the deposition can meet its burden of persuasion under this rule. The burden to persuade the court that the officer is high-level for purposes of this rule lies with the person or party opposing the deposition.

(i) **Form of Responses to Written Discovery Requests**. When responding to requests for production served pursuant to rule 1.310(b)(5), written deposition questions served pursuant to rule 1.320, interrogatories served pursuant to rule 1.340, requests for production or inspection served pursuant to rule 1.350, requests for production of documents or things without deposition served pursuant to rule 1.351, requests for admissions served pursuant to rule 1.370, or requests for the production of documentary evidence served pursuant to rule 1.410(c), the responding party shall state each deposition question, interrogatory, or discovery request in full as numbered, followed by the answer, objection, or other response.

Rule 1.285 Inadvertent Disclosure of Privileged Materials

(a) **Assertion of Privilege as to Inadvertently Disclosed Materials**. Any party, person, or entity, after inadvertent disclosure of any materials pursuant to these rules, may thereafter assert any privilege recognized by law as to those materials. This right exists without regard to whether the disclosure was made pursuant to formal demand or informal request. In order to assert the privilege, the party, person, or entity, shall, within 10 days of actually discovering the inadvertent disclosure, serve written notice of the assertion of privilege on the party to whom the materials were disclosed. The notice shall specify with particularity the materials as to which the privilege is asserted, the nature of the privilege asserted, and the date on which the inadvertent disclosure was actually discovered.

(b) **Duty of the Party Receiving Notice of an Assertion of Privilege**. A party receiving notice of an assertion of privilege under subdivision (a) shall promptly return, sequester, or destroy the materials specified in the notice, as well as any copies of the material. The party receiving the notice shall also promptly notify any other party, person, or entity to whom it has disclosed the materials of the fact that the notice has been served and of the effect of this rule. That party shall also take reasonable steps to retrieve the materials disclosed. Nothing herein affects any obligation pursuant to R. Regulating Fla. Bar 4-4.4(b).

(c) **Right to Challenge Assertion of Privilege**. Any party receiving a notice made under subdivision (a) has the right to challenge the assertion of privilege. The grounds for the challenge may include, but are not limited to, the following:

(1)   The materials in question are not privileged.

(2)   The disclosing party, person, or entity lacks standing to assert the privilege.

(3)   The disclosing party, person, or entity has failed to serve timely notice under this rule.

(4)   The circumstances surrounding the production or disclosure of the materials warrant a finding that the disclosing party, person, or entity has waived its assertion that the material is protected by a privilege.

Any party seeking to challenge the assertion of privilege shall do so by serving notice of its challenge on the party, person, or entity asserting the privilege. Notice of the challenge shall be served within 20 days of service of the original notice given by the disclosing party, person, or entity. The notice of the recipient's challenge shall specify the grounds for the challenge. Failure to serve timely notice of challenge is a waiver of the right to challenge.

(d) **Effect of Determination that Privilege Applies**. When an order is entered determining that materials are privileged or that the right to challenge the privilege has been waived, the court shall direct what shall be done with the materials and any copies so as to preserve all rights of appellate review. The recipient of the materials shall also give prompt notice of the court's determination to any other party, person, or entity to whom it had disclosed the materials.

Rule 1.290 Depositions Before Action or Pending Appeal

(a) **Before Action**.

(1)   *Petition*. A person who desires to perpetuate that person's own testimony or that of another person regarding any matter that may be cognizable in any court of this state may file a verified petition in the circuit court in the county of the residence of any expected adverse party. The petition shall be entitled in the name of the petitioner and shall show: (1) that the petitioner expects to be a party to an action cognizable in a court of Florida, but is presently unable to bring it or cause it to be brought, (2) the subject matter of the expected action and the petitioner's interest therein, (3) the facts which the petitioner desires to establish by the proposed testimony and the petitioner's reasons for desiring to perpetuate it, (4) the names or a description of the persons the petitioner expects will be adverse parties and their addresses so far as known, and (5) the names and addresses of the persons to be examined and the substance of the testimony which the petitioner expects to elicit from each; and shall ask for an order authorizing the petitioner to take the deposition of the persons to be examined named in the petition for the purpose of perpetuating their testimony.

(2)   *Notice and Service*. The petitioner shall thereafter serve a notice upon each person named in the petition as an expected adverse party, together with a copy of the petition, stating that the petitioner will apply to the court at a time and place named therein for an order described in the petition. At least 20 days before the date of hearing the notice shall be served either within or without the county in the manner provided by law for service of summons, but if such service cannot with due diligence be made upon any expected adverse party named in the petition, the court may make an order for service by publication or otherwise, and shall appoint an attorney for persons not served in the manner provided by law for service of summons who shall represent them, and if they are not otherwise represented, shall cross-examine the deponent.

(3)   *Order and Examination*. If the court is satisfied that the perpetuation of the testimony may prevent a failure or delay of justice, it shall make an order designating or describing the persons whose depositions may be taken and specifying the subject matter of the examination and whether the deposition shall be taken upon oral examination or written interrogatories. The deposition may then be taken in accordance with these rules and the court may make orders in accordance with the

requirements of these rules. For the purpose of applying these rules to depositions for perpetuating testimony, each reference therein to the court in which the action is pending shall be deemed to refer to the court in which the petition for such deposition was filed.

(4) *Use of Deposition*. A deposition taken under this rule may be used in any action involving the same subject matter subsequently brought in any court in accordance with rule 1.330.

(b) **Pending Appeal**. If an appeal has been taken from a judgment of any court or before the taking of an appeal if the time therefor has not expired, the court in which the judgment was rendered may allow the taking of the depositions of witnesses to perpetuate their testimony for use in the event of further proceedings in the court. In such case the party who desires to perpetuate the testimony may make a motion for leave to take the deposition upon the same notice and service as if the action was pending in the court. The motion shall show (1) the names and addresses of persons to be examined and the substance of the testimony which the movant expects to elicit from each, and (2) the reason for perpetuating their testimony. If the court finds that the perpetuation of the testimony is proper to avoid a failure or delay in justice, it may make an order allowing the deposition to be taken and may make orders of the character provided for by these rules, and thereupon the deposition may be taken and used in the same manner and under the same conditions as are prescribed in these rules for depositions taken in actions pending in the court.

(c) **Perpetuation by Action**. This rule does not limit the power of a court to entertain an action to perpetuate testimony.

Rule 1.300 Persons Before Whom Depositions May Be Taken

(a) **Persons Authorized**. Depositions may be taken before any notary public or judicial officer or before any officer authorized by the statutes of Florida to take acknowledgments or proof of executions of deeds or by any person appointed by the court in which the action is pending.

(b) **In Foreign Countries**. In a foreign country depositions may be taken (1) on notice before a person authorized to administer oaths in the place in which the examination is held, either by the law thereof or by the law of Florida or of the United States, (2) before a person commissioned by the court, and a person so commissioned shall have the power by virtue of the commission to administer any necessary oath and take testimony, or (3) pursuant to a letter rogatory. A commission or a letter rogatory shall be issued on application and notice and on terms that are just and appropriate. It is not requisite to the issuance of a commission or a letter rogatory that the taking of the deposition in any other manner is impracticable or inconvenient, and both a commission and a letter rogatory may be issued in proper cases. A notice or commission may designate the person before whom the deposition is to be taken either by name or descriptive title. A letter rogatory may be addressed "To the Appropriate Authority in ..... (name of country) ...... " Evidence obtained in response to a letter rogatory need not be excluded merely for the reason that it is not a verbatim transcript or that the testimony was not taken under oath or any similar departure from the requirements for depositions taken within Florida under these rules.

(c) **Selection by Stipulation**. If the parties so stipulate in writing, depositions may be taken before any person at any time or place upon any notice and in any manner and when so taken may be used like other depositions.

(d) **Persons Disqualified**. Unless so stipulated by the parties, no deposition shall be taken before a person who is a relative, employee, attorney, or counsel of any of the parties, is a relative or employee of any of the parties' attorney or counsel, or is financially interested in the action.

Rule 1.310 Depositions Upon Oral Examination

(a) **When Depositions May Be Taken**. After commencement of the action any party may take the testimony of any person, including a party, by deposition upon oral examination. Leave of court, granted with or without notice, must be obtained only if the plaintiff seeks to take a deposition within 30 days after service of the process and initial pleading on any defendant, except that leave is not required (1) if a defendant has served a notice of taking deposition or otherwise sought discovery, or (2) if special notice is given as provided in subdivision (b)(2) of this rule. The attendance of witnesses may be compelled by subpoena as provided in rule 1.410. The deposition of a person confined in prison may be taken only by leave of court on such terms as the court prescribes.

(b) Notice; Method of Taking; Production at Deposition.

(1) A party desiring to take the deposition of any person on oral examination must give reasonable notice in writing to every other party to the action. The notice must state the time and place for taking the deposition and the name and address of each person to be examined, if known, and, if the name is not known, a general description sufficient to identify the person or the particular class or group to which the person belongs. If a subpoena duces tecum is to be served on the person to be examined, the designation of the materials to be produced under the subpoena must be attached to or included in the notice.

(2) Leave of court is not required for the taking of a deposition by plaintiff if the notice states that the person to be examined is about to go out of the state and will be unavailable for examination unless a deposition is taken before expiration of the 30-day period under subdivision (a). If a party shows that when served with notice under this subdivision that party was unable through the exercise of diligence to obtain counsel to represent the party at the taking of the deposition, the deposition may not be used against that party.

(3) For cause shown the court may enlarge or shorten the time for taking the deposition.

(4) Any deposition may be recorded by videotape without leave of the court or stipulation of the parties, provided the deposition is taken in accordance with this subdivision.

 (A) Notice. A party intending to videotape a deposition must state in the notice that the deposition is to be videotaped and must give the name and address of the operator. Any subpoena served on the person to be examined must state the method or methods for recording the testimony.

 (B) Stenographer. Videotaped depositions must also be recorded stenographically, unless all parties agree otherwise.

 (C) Procedure. At the beginning of the deposition, the officer before whom it is taken must, on camera:

  (i) identify the style of the action,

  (ii) state the date, and

  (iii) swear the witness.

 (D) Custody of Tape and Copies . The attorney for the party requesting the videotaping of the deposition must take custody of and be responsible for the safeguarding of the videotape, must permit the viewing of it by the opposing party, and, if requested, must provide a copy of the videotape at the expense of the party requesting the copy.

 (E) Cost of Videotaped Depositions. The party requesting the videotaping must bear the initial cost of videotaping.

(5) The notice to a party deponent may be accompanied by a request made in compliance with rule 1.350 for the production of documents and tangible things at the taking of the deposition. The procedure of rule 1.350 applies to the request. Rule 1.351 provides the exclusive procedure for obtaining documents or things by subpoena from nonparties without deposing the custodian or other person in possession of the documents.

(6) In the notice a party may name as the deponent a public or private corporation, a partnership or association, or a governmental agency, and designate with reasonable particularity the matters on which examination is requested. The organization so named must designate one or more officers, directors, or managing agents, or other persons who consent to do so, to testify on its behalf and may state the matters on which each person designated will testify. The persons so designated must testify about matters known or reasonably available to the organization. This subdivision does not preclude taking a deposition by any other procedure authorized in these rules.

(7) On motion the court may order that the testimony at a deposition be taken by telephone. The order may prescribe the manner in which the deposition will be taken. A party may also arrange for a stenographic transcription at that party's own initial expense.

(8) Any minor subpoenaed for testimony has the right to be accompanied by a parent or guardian at all times during the taking of testimony notwithstanding the invocation of the rule of sequestration of section 90.616, Florida Statutes, except on a showing that the presence of a parent or guardian is likely to have a material, negative impact on the credibility or accuracy of the minor's testimony, or that the interests of the parent or guardian are in actual or potential conflict with the interests of the minor.

(c) **Examination and Cross-Examination; Record of Examination; Oath; Objections**. Examination and cross-examination of witnesses may proceed as permitted at the trial. The officer before whom the deposition is to be taken must put the witness on oath and must personally, or by someone acting under the officer's direction and in the officer's presence, record the testimony of the witness, except that when a deposition is being taken by telephone, the witness must be sworn by a person present with the witness who is qualified to administer an oath in that location. The testimony must be taken stenographically or recorded by any other means ordered in accordance with subdivision (b)(4) of this rule. If requested by one of the parties, the testimony must be transcribed at the initial cost of the requesting party and prompt notice of the request must be given to all other parties. All objections made at time of the examination to the qualifications of the officer taking the deposition, the manner of taking it, the evidence presented, or the conduct of any party, and any other objection to the proceedings must be noted by the officer on the deposition. Any objection during a deposition must be stated concisely and in a nonargumentative and nonsuggestive manner. A party may instruct a deponent not to answer only when necessary to preserve a privilege, to enforce a limitation on evidence directed by the court, or to present a motion under subdivision (d). Otherwise, evidence objected to must be taken subject to the objections. Instead of participating in the oral examination, parties may serve written questions in a sealed envelope on the party taking the deposition and that party must transmit them to the officer, who must propound them to the witness and record the answers verbatim.

(d) **Motion to Terminate or Limit Examination**. At any time during the taking of the deposition, on motion of a party or of the deponent and on a showing that the examination is being conducted in bad faith or in such manner as unreasonably to annoy, embarrass, or oppress the deponent or party, or that objection and instruction to a deponent not to answer are being made in violation of rule 1.310(c), the court in which the action is pending or the circuit court where the deposition is being taken may order the officer conducting the examination to cease immediately from taking the deposition or may limit the scope and manner of the taking of the deposition under rule 1.280(c). If the order terminates the examination, it shall be resumed thereafter only on the order of the court in which the action is pending. Upon demand of any party or the deponent, the taking of the deposition must be suspended for the time necessary to make a motion for an order. The provisions of rule 1.380(a) apply to the award of expenses incurred in relation to the motion.

(e) **Witness Review**. If the testimony is transcribed, the transcript must be furnished to the witness for examination and must be read to or by the witness unless the examination and reading are waived by the witness and by the parties. Any changes in form or substance that the witness wants to make must be listed in writing by the officer with a statement of the reasons given by the witness for making the changes. The changes must be attached to the transcript. It must then be signed by the witness unless the parties waived the signing or the witness is ill, cannot be found, or refuses to sign. If the transcript is not signed by the witness within a reasonable time after it is furnished to the witness, the officer must sign the transcript and state on the transcript the waiver, illness, absence of the witness, or refusal to sign with any reasons given therefor. The deposition may then be used as fully as though signed unless the court holds that the reasons given for the refusal to sign require rejection of the deposition wholly or partly, on motion under rule 1.330(d)(4).

(f) **Filing; Exhibits.**

(1) If the deposition is transcribed, the officer must certify on each copy of the deposition that the witness was duly sworn by the officer and that the deposition is a true record of the testimony given by the witness. Documents and things produced for inspection during the examination of the witness must be marked for identification and annexed to and returned with the deposition on the request of a party, and may be inspected and copied by any party, except that the person producing the materials may substitute copies to be marked for identification if that person affords to all parties fair opportunity to verify the copies by comparison with the originals. If the person producing the materials requests their return, the officer must mark them, give each party an opportunity to inspect and copy them, and return them to the person producing them and the materials may then be used in the same manner as if annexed to and returned with the deposition.

(2) Upon payment of reasonable charges therefor the officer must furnish a copy of the deposition to any party or to the deponent.

(3) A copy of a deposition may be filed only under the following circumstances:

(A) It may be filed in compliance with Florida Rule of General Practice and Judicial Administration 2.425 and rule 1.280(g) by a party or the witness when the contents of the deposition must be considered by the court on any matter pending before the court. Prompt notice of the filing of the deposition must be given to all parties unless notice is waived. A party filing the deposition must furnish a copy of the deposition or the part being filed to other parties unless the party already has a copy.

(B) If the court determines that a deposition previously taken is necessary for the decision of a matter pending before the court, the court may order that a copy be filed by any party at the initial cost of the party, and the filing party must comply with rules 2.425 and 1.280(g).

(g) **Obtaining Copies**. A party or witness who does not have a copy of the deposition may obtain it from the officer taking the deposition unless the court orders otherwise. If the deposition is obtained from a person other than the officer, the reasonable cost of reproducing the copies must be paid to the person by the requesting party or witness.

(h) **Failure to Attend or to Serve Subpoena; Expenses**.

(1) If the party giving the notice of the taking of a deposition fails to attend and proceed therewith and another party attends in person or by attorney pursuant to the notice, the court may order the party giving the notice to pay to the other party the reasonable expenses incurred by the other party and the other party's attorney in attending, including reasonable attorneys' fees.

(2) If the party giving the notice of the taking of a deposition of a witness fails to serve a subpoena on the witness and the witness because of the failure does not attend and if another party attends in person or by attorney because that other party expects the deposition of that witness to be taken, the court may order the party giving the notice to pay to the other party the reasonable expenses incurred by that other party and that other party's attorney in attending, including reasonable attorneys' fees.

Rule 1.320 Depositions Upon Written Questions

(a) **Serving Questions; Notice**. After commencement of the action any party may take the testimony of any person, including a party, by deposition upon written questions. The attendance of witnesses may be compelled by the use of subpoena as provided in rule 1.410. The deposition of a person confined in prison may be taken only by leave of court on such terms as the court prescribes. A party desiring to take a deposition upon written questions shall serve them with a notice stating (1) the name and address of the person who is to answer them, if known, and, if the name is not known, a general description sufficient to identify the person or the particular class or group to which that person belongs, and (2) the name or descriptive title and address of the officer before whom the deposition is to be taken. A deposition upon written questions may be taken of a public or private corporation, a partnership or association, or a governmental agency in accordance with rule 1.310(b)(6). Within 30 days after the notice and written questions are served, a party may serve cross questions upon all other parties. Within 10 days after being served with cross questions, a party may serve redirect questions upon all other parties. Within 10 days after being served with redirect questions, a party may serve recross questions upon all other parties. The court may for cause shown enlarge or shorten the time.

(b) **Officer to Take Responses and Prepare Record**. A copy of the notice and copies of all questions served shall be delivered by the party taking the depositions to the officer designated in the notice, who shall proceed promptly to take the testimony of the witness in the manner provided by rules 1.310(c), (e), and (f) in response to the questions and to prepare the deposition, attaching the copy of the notice and the questions received by the officer. The questions shall not be filed separately from the deposition unless a party seeks to have the court consider the questions before the questions are submitted to the witness.

Rule 1.330 Use of Depositions in Court Proceedings

(a) **Use of Depositions**. At the trial or upon the hearing of a motion or an interlocutory proceeding, any part or all of a deposition may be used against any party who was present or represented at the taking of the deposition or who had reasonable notice of it so far as admissible under the rules of evidence applied as though the witness were then present and testifying in accordance with any of the following provisions:

(1) Any deposition may be used by any party for the purpose of contradicting or impeaching the testimony of the deponent as a witness or for any purpose permitted by the Florida Evidence Code.

(2)   The deposition of a party or of anyone who at the time of taking the deposition was an officer, director, or managing agent or a person designated under rule 1.310(b)(6) or 1.320(a) to testify on behalf of a public or private corporation, a partnership or association, or a governmental agency that is a party may be used by an adverse party for any purpose.

(3)   The deposition of a witness, whether or not a party, may be used by any party for any purpose if the court finds: (A) that the witness is dead; (B) that the witness is at a greater distance than 100 miles from the place of trial or hearing, or is out of the state, unless it appears that the absence of the witness was procured by the party offering the deposition; (C) that the witness is unable to attend or testify because of age, illness, infirmity, or imprisonment; (D) that the party offering the deposition has been unable to procure the attendance of the witness by subpoena; (E) upon application and notice, that such exceptional circumstances exist as to make it desirable, in the interest of justice and with due regard to the importance of presenting the testimony of witnesses orally in open court, to allow the deposition to be used; or (F) the witness is an expert or skilled witness.

(4)   If only part of a deposition is offered in evidence by a party, an adverse party may require the party to introduce any other part that in fairness ought to be considered with the part introduced, and any party may introduce any other parts.

(5)   Substitution of parties pursuant to rule 1.260 does not affect the right to use depositions previously taken and, when an action in any court of the United States or of any state has been dismissed and another action involving the same subject matter is afterward brought between the same parties or their representatives or successors in interest, all depositions lawfully taken and duly filed in the former action may be used in the latter as if originally taken for it.

(6)   If a civil action is afterward brought, all depositions lawfully taken in a medical liability mediation proceeding may be used in the civil action as if originally taken for it.

(b)   **Objections to Admissibility**. Subject to the provisions of rule 1.300(b) and subdivision (d)(3) of this rule, objection may be made at the trial or hearing to receiving in evidence any deposition or part of it for any reason that would require the exclusion of the evidence if the witness were then present and testifying.

(c)   **Effect of Taking or Using Depositions**. A party does not make a person the party's own witness for any purpose by taking the person's deposition. The introduction in evidence of the deposition or any part of it for any purpose other than that of contradicting or impeaching the deponent makes the deponent the witness of the party introducing the deposition, but this shall not apply to the use by an adverse party of a deposition under subdivision (a)(2) of this rule. At the trial or hearing any party may rebut any relevant evidence contained in a deposition whether introduced by that party or by any other party.

(d)   **Effect of Errors and Irregularities**.

(1)   *As to Notice*. All errors and irregularities in the notice for taking a deposition are waived unless written objection is promptly served upon the party giving the notice.

(2)   *As to Disqualification of Officer*. Objection to taking a deposition because of disqualification of the officer before whom it is to be taken is waived unless made before the taking of the deposition begins or as soon thereafter as the disqualification becomes known or could be discovered with reasonable diligence.

(3)   *As to Taking of Deposition*.

(A)   Objections to the competency of a witness or to the competency, relevancy, or materiality of testimony are not waived by failure to make them before or during the taking of the deposition unless the ground of the objection is one that might have been obviated or removed if presented at that time.

(B)   Errors and irregularities occurring at the oral examination in the manner of taking the deposition, in the form of the questions or answers, in the oath or affirmation, or in the conduct of parties and errors of any kind that might be obviated, removed, or cured if promptly presented are waived unless timely objection to them is made at the taking of the deposition.

(C)   Objections to the form of written questions submitted under rule 1.320 are waived unless served in writing upon the party propounding them within the time allowed for serving the succeeding cross or other questions and within 10 days after service of the last questions authorized.

(4) *As to Completion and Return.* Errors and irregularities in the manner in which the testimony is transcribed or the deposition is prepared, signed, certified, or otherwise dealt with by the officer under rules 1.310 and 1.320 are waived unless a motion to suppress the deposition or some part of it is made with reasonable promptness after the defect is, or with due diligence might have been, discovered.

Rule 1.340 Interrogatories to Parties

(a) **Procedure for Use**. Without leave of court, any party may serve on any other party written interrogatories to be answered (1) by the party to whom the interrogatories are directed, or (2) if that party is a public or private corporation or partnership or association or governmental agency, by any officer or agent, who must furnish the information available to that party. Interrogatories may be served on the plaintiff after commencement of the action and on any other party with or after service of the process and initial pleading on that party. The interrogatories must not exceed 30, including all subparts, unless the court permits a larger number on motion and notice and for good cause. If the supreme court has approved a form of interrogatories for the type of action, the initial interrogatories on a subject included within must be from the form approved by the court. A party may serve fewer than all of the approved interrogatories within a form. Other interrogatories may be added to the approved forms without leave of court, so long as the total of approved and additional interrogatories does not exceed 30. Each interrogatory must be answered separately and fully in writing under oath unless it is objected to, in which event the grounds for objection must be stated and signed by the attorney making it. The party to whom the interrogatories are directed must serve the answers and any objections within 30 days after the service of the interrogatories, except that a defendant may serve answers or objections within 45 days after service of the process and initial pleading on that defendant. The court may allow a shorter or longer time. The party submitting the interrogatories may move for an order under rule 1.380(a) on any objection to or other failure to answer an interrogatory.

(b) **Scope; Use at Trial**. Interrogatories may relate to any matters that can be inquired into under rule 1.280(b), and the answers may be used to the extent permitted by the rules of evidence except as otherwise provided in this subdivision. An interrogatory otherwise proper is not objectionable merely because an answer to the interrogatory involves an opinion or contention that relates to fact or calls for a conclusion or asks for information not within the personal knowledge of the party. A party must respond to such an interrogatory by giving the information the party has and the source on which the information is based. Such a qualified answer may not be used as direct evidence for or impeachment against the party giving the answer unless the court finds it otherwise admissible under the rules of evidence. If a party introduces an answer to an interrogatory, any other party may require that party to introduce any other interrogatory and answer that in fairness ought to be considered with it.

(c) **Option to Produce Records**. When the answer to an interrogatory may be derived or ascertained from the records (including electronically stored information) of the party to whom the interrogatory is directed or from an examination, audit, or inspection of the records or from a compilation, abstract, or summary based on the records and the burden of deriving or ascertaining the answer is substantially the same for the party serving the interrogatory as for the party to whom it is directed, an answer to the interrogatory specifying the records from which the answer may be derived or ascertained and offering to give the party serving the interrogatory a reasonable opportunity to examine, audit, or inspect the records and to make copies, compilations, abstracts, or summaries is a sufficient answer. An answer must be in sufficient detail to permit the interrogating party to locate and to identify, as readily as can the party interrogated, the records from which the answer may be derived or ascertained, or must identify a person or persons representing the interrogated party who will be available to assist the interrogating party in locating and identifying the records at the time they are produced. If the records to be produced consist of electronically stored information, the records must be produced in a form or forms in which they are ordinarily maintained or in a reasonably usable form or forms.

(d) **Effect on Co-Party**. Answers made by a party shall not be binding on a co-party.

(e) **Service and Filing**. Interrogatories must be served on the party to whom the interrogatories are directed and copies must be served on all other parties. A certificate of service of the interrogatories must be filed, giving the date of service and the name of the party to whom they were directed. The answers to the interrogatories must be served on the party originally propounding the interrogatories and a copy must be served on all other parties by the answering party. The original or any copy of the answers to interrogatories may be filed in compliance with Florida Rule of General Practice Judicial Administration 2.425 and rule 1.280(g) by any party when the court should consider the answers to interrogatories in determining any matter pending before the court. The court may order a copy of the answers to interrogatories filed at any time when the court determines that examination of the answers to interrogatories is necessary to determine any matter pending before the court.

Rule 1.350 Production of Documents and Things and Entry Upon Land for Inspection and Other Purposes

(a) **Request; Scope**. Any party may request any other party (1) to produce and permit the party making the request, or someone acting in the requesting party's behalf, to inspect and copy any designated documents, including electronically stored information, writings, drawings, graphs, charts, photographs, audio, visual, and audiovisual recordings, and other data compilations from which information can be obtained, translated, if necessary, by the party to whom the request is directed through detection devices into reasonably usable form, that constitute or contain matters within the scope of rule 1.280(b) and that are in the possession, custody, or control of the party to whom the request is directed; (2) to inspect and copy, test, or sample any tangible things that constitute or contain matters within the scope of rule 1.280(b) and that are in the possession, custody, or control of the party to whom the request is directed; or (3) to permit entry upon designated land or other property in the possession or control of the party upon whom the request is served for the purpose of inspection and measuring, surveying, photographing, testing, or sampling the property or any designated object or operation on it within the scope of rule 1.280(b).

(b) **Procedure**. Without leave of court the request may be served on the plaintiff after commencement of the action and on any other party with or after service of the process and initial pleading on that party. The request shall set forth the items to be inspected, either by individual item or category, and describe each item and category with reasonable particularity. The request shall specify a reasonable time, place, and manner of making the inspection or performing the related acts. The party to whom the request is directed shall serve a written response within 30 days after service of the request, except that a defendant may serve a response within 45 days after service of the process and initial pleading on that defendant. The court may allow a shorter or longer time. For each item or category the response shall state that inspection and related activities will be permitted as requested unless the request is objected to, in which event the reasons for the objection shall be stated. If an objection is made to part of an item or category, the part shall be specified. When producing documents, the producing party shall either produce them as they are kept in the usual course of business or shall identify them to correspond with the categories in the request. A request for electronically stored information may specify the form or forms in which electronically stored information is to be produced. If the responding party objects to a requested form, or if no form is specified in the request, the responding party must state the form or forms it intends to use. If a request for electronically stored information does not specify the form of production, the producing party must produce the information in a form or forms in which it is ordinarily maintained or in a reasonably usable form or forms. The party submitting the request may move for an order under rule 1.380 concerning any objection, failure to respond to the request, or any part of it, or failure to permit the inspection as requested.

(c) **Persons Not Parties**. This rule does not preclude an independent action against a person not a party for production of documents and things and permission to enter upon land.

(d) **Filing of Documents**. Unless required by the court, a party shall not file any of the documents or things produced with the response. Documents or things may be filed in compliance with Florida Rule of General Practice and Judicial Administration 2.425 and rule 1.280(g) when they should be considered by the court in determining a matter pending before the court.

Rule 1.351 Production of Documents and Things Without Deposition

(a) **Request; Scope**. A party may seek inspection and copying of any documents or things within the scope of rule 1.350(a) from a person who is not a party by issuance of a subpoena directing the production of the documents or things when the requesting party does not seek to depose the custodian or other person in possession of the documents or things. This rule provides the exclusive procedure for obtaining documents or things by subpoena from nonparties without deposing the custodian or other person in possession of the documents or things pursuant to rule 1.310.

(b) **Procedure**. A party desiring production under this rule shall serve notice as provided in Florida Rule of General Practice and Judicial Administration 2.516 on every other party of the intent to serve a subpoena under this rule at least 10 days before the subpoena is issued if service is by delivery or e-mail and 15 days before the subpoena is issued if the service is by mail. The proposed subpoena shall be attached to the notice and shall state the time, place, and method for production of the documents or things, and the name and address of the person who is to produce the documents or things, if known, and if not known, a general description sufficient to identify the person or the particular class or group to which the person belongs; shall include a designation of the items to be produced; and shall state that the person who will be asked to produce the documents or things has the right to object to the production under this rule and that the person will not be required to surrender the documents or things. A copy of the notice and proposed subpoena shall not be furnished to the person upon whom the subpoena is to be served. If any party serves an objection to production under this rule within 10 days of service of the notice, the documents or things shall not be produced pending resolution of the objection in accordance with subdivision (d).

(c) **Subpoena**. If no objection is made by a party under subdivision (b), an attorney of record in the action may issue a subpoena or the party desiring production shall deliver to the clerk for issuance a subpoena together with a certificate of counsel or pro se party that no timely objection has been received from any party, and the clerk shall issue the subpoena and deliver it to the party desiring production. Service within the state of Florida of a nonparty subpoena shall be deemed sufficient if it complies with rule 1.410(d) or if (1) service is accomplished by mail or hand delivery by a commercial delivery service, and (2) written confirmation of delivery, with the date of service and the name and signature of the person accepting the subpoena, is obtained and filed by the party seeking production. The subpoena shall be identical to the copy attached to the notice and shall specify that no testimony may be taken and shall require only production of the documents or things specified in it. The subpoena may give the recipient an option to deliver or mail legible copies of the documents or things to the party serving the subpoena. The person upon whom the subpoena is served may condition the preparation of copies on the payment in advance of the reasonable costs of preparing the copies. The subpoena shall require production only in the county of the residence of the custodian or other person in possession of the documents or things or in the county where the documents or things are located or where the custodian or person in possession usually conducts business. If the person upon whom the subpoena is served objects at any time before the production of the documents or things, the documents or things shall not be produced under this rule, and relief may be obtained pursuant to rule 1.310.

(d) **Ruling on Objection**. If an objection is made by a party under subdivision (b), the party desiring production may file a motion with the court seeking a ruling on the objection or may proceed pursuant to rule 1.310.

(e) **Copies Furnished**. If the subpoena is complied with by delivery or mailing of copies as provided in subdivision (c), the party receiving the copies shall furnish a legible copy of each item furnished to any other party who requests it upon the payment of the reasonable cost of preparing the copies.

(f) **Independent Action**. This rule does not affect the right of any party to bring an independent action for production of documents and things or permission to enter upon land.

Rule 1.360 Examination of Persons

(a) **Request; Scope**.
    (1) A party may request any other party to submit to, or to produce a person in that other party's custody or legal control for, examination by a qualified expert when the condition that is the subject of the requested examination is in controversy.
        (A) When the physical condition of a party or other person under subdivision (a)(1) is in controversy, the request may be served on the plaintiff without leave of court after commencement of the action, and on any other person with or after service of the process and initial pleading on that party. The request shall specify a reasonable time, place, manner, conditions, and scope of the examination and the person or persons by whom the examination

is to be made. The party to whom the request is directed shall serve a response within 30 days after service of the request, except that a defendant need not serve a response until 45 days after service of the process and initial pleading on that defendant. The court may allow a shorter or longer time. The response shall state that the examination will be permitted as requested unless the request is objected to, in which event the reasons for the objection shall be stated. If the examination is to be recorded or observed by others, the request or response shall also include the number of people attending, their role, and the method or methods of recording.

    (B) In cases where the condition in controversy is not physical, a party may move for an examination by a qualified expert as in subdivision (a)(1). The order for examination shall be made only after notice to the person to be examined and to all parties, and shall specify the time, place, manner, conditions, and scope of the examination and the person or persons by whom it is to be made.

    (C) Any minor required to submit to examination pursuant to this rule shall have the right to be accompanied by a parent or guardian at all times during the examination, except upon a showing that the presence of a parent or guardian is likely to have a material, negative impact on the minor's examination.

  (2) An examination under this rule is authorized only when the party submitting the request has good cause for the examination. At any hearing the party submitting the request shall have the burden of showing good cause.

  (3) Upon request of either the party requesting the examination or the party or person to be examined, the court may establish protective rules governing such examination.

(b) **Report of Examiner**.

  (1) If requested by the party to whom a request for examination or against whom an order is made under subdivision (a)(1)(A) or (a)(1)(B) or by the person examined, the party requesting the examination to be made shall deliver to the other party a copy of a detailed written report of the examiner setting out the examiner's findings, including results of all tests made, diagnosis, and conclusions, with similar reports of all earlier examinations of the same condition. After delivery of the detailed written report, the party requesting the examination to be made shall be entitled upon request to receive from the party to whom the request for examination or against whom the order is made a similar report of any examination of the same condition previously or thereafter made, unless in the case of a report of examination of a person not a party the party shows the inability to obtain it. On motion, the court may order delivery of a report on such terms as are just; and if an examiner fails or refuses to make a report, the court may exclude the examiner's testimony if offered at the trial.

  (2) By requesting and obtaining a report of the examination so ordered or requested or by taking the deposition of the examiner, the party examined waives any privilege that party may have in that action or any other involving the same controversy regarding the testimony of every other person who has examined or may thereafter examine that party concerning the same condition.

  (3) This subdivision applies to examinations made by agreement of the parties unless the agreement provides otherwise. This subdivision does not preclude discovery of a report of an examiner or taking the deposition of the examiner in accordance with any other rule.

(c) **Examiner as Witness**. The examiner may be called as a witness by any party to the action, but shall not be identified as appointed by the court.

Rule 1.370 Requests for Admission

(a) **Request for Admission**. A party may serve upon any other party a written request for the admission of the truth of any matters within the scope of rule 1.280(b) set forth in the request that relate to statements or opinions of fact or of the application of law to fact, including the genuineness of any documents described in the request. Copies of documents shall be served with the request unless they have been or are otherwise furnished or made available for inspection and copying. Without leave of court the request may be served upon the plaintiff after commencement of the action and upon any other party with or after service of the process and initial pleading upon that party. The request for admission shall not exceed 30 requests, including all subparts, unless the court permits a larger number on motion and notice and for good cause, or the parties propounding and responding to the requests stipulate to a larger number. Each matter of which an admission is requested shall be separately set forth. The matter is admitted unless the party to whom the request is directed serves upon the party requesting the admission a written answer or objection addressed to the matter within 30 days after service of the request or such shorter or longer time as the court may allow but, unless the court shortens the time, a defendant shall not be required to serve answers or objections before the expiration of 45 days after service of the process and initial pleading upon the defendant. If objection is made, the reasons shall be stated. The answer shall specifically deny the matter or set forth in detail the reasons why the answering party cannot truthfully admit or deny the matter. A denial shall fairly meet the substance of the requested admission, and when good faith requires that a party qualify an answer or deny only a part of the matter of which an admission is requested, the party shall specify so much of it as is true and qualify or deny the remainder. An answering party may not give lack of information or knowledge as a reason for failure to admit or deny unless that party states that that party has made reasonable inquiry and that the information known or readily obtainable by that party is insufficient to enable that party to admit or deny. A party who considers that a matter of which an admission has been requested presents a genuine issue for trial may not object to the request on that ground alone; the party may deny the matter or set forth reasons why the party cannot admit or deny it, subject to rule 1.380(c). The party who has requested the admissions may move to determine the sufficiency of the answers or objections. Unless the court determines that an objection is justified, it shall order that an answer be served. If the court determines that an answer does not comply with the requirements of this rule, it may order either that the matter is admitted or that an amended answer be served. Instead of these orders the court may determine that final disposition of the request be made at a pretrial conference or at a designated time before trial. The provisions of rule 1.380(a)(4) apply to the award of expenses incurred in relation to the motion.

(b) **Effect of Admission**. Any matter admitted under this rule is conclusively established unless the court on motion permits withdrawal or amendment of the admission. Subject to rule 1.200 governing amendment of a pretrial order, the court may permit withdrawal or amendment when the presentation of the merits of the action will be subserved by it and the party who obtained the admission fails to satisfy the court that withdrawal or amendment will prejudice that party in maintaining an action or defense on the merits. Any admission made by a party under this rule is for the purpose of the pending action only and is not an admission for any other purpose nor may it be used against that party in any other proceeding.

Rule 1.380 Failure to Make Discovery; Sanctions

(a) **Motion for Order Compelling Discovery**. Upon reasonable notice to other parties and all persons affected, a party may apply for an order compelling discovery as follows:

(1) *Appropriate Court*. An application for an order to a party may be made to the court in which the action is pending or in accordance with rule 1.310(d). An application for an order to a deponent who is not a party shall be made to the circuit court where the deposition is being taken.

(2) *Motion*. If a deponent fails to answer a question propounded or submitted under rule 1.310 or 1.320, or a corporation or other entity fails to make a designation under rule 1.310(b)(6) or 1.320(a), or a party fails to answer an interrogatory submitted under rule 1.340, or if a party in response to a request for inspection submitted under rule 1.350 fails to respond that inspection will be permitted as requested or fails to permit inspection as requested, or if a party in response to a request for examination of a person submitted under rule 1.360(a) objects to the examination, fails to respond that the examination will be permitted as requested, or fails to submit to or to produce a person in that party's custody or legal control for examination, the discovering party may move for an order compelling an answer, or a designation or an order compelling inspection, or an order compelling an examination in accordance with the request. The motion must include a certification that the movant, in good faith, has conferred or attempted to confer with the person or party failing to make the discovery in an effort to secure the information or material without court action. When taking a deposition on oral examination, the proponent of the question may complete or adjourn the examination before applying for an order. If the court denies the motion in whole or in part, it may make such protective order as it would have been empowered to make on a motion made pursuant to rule 1.280(c).

(3) *Evasive or Incomplete Answer.* For purposes of this subdivision an evasive or incomplete answer shall be treated as a failure to answer.

(4) *Award of Expenses of Motion.* If the motion is granted and after opportunity for hearing, the court shall require the party or deponent whose conduct necessitated the motion or the party or counsel advising the conduct to pay to the moving party the reasonable expenses incurred in obtaining the order that may include attorneys' fees, unless the court finds that the movant failed to certify in the motion that a good faith effort was made to obtain the discovery without court action, that the opposition to the motion was substantially justified, or that other circumstances make an award of expenses unjust. If the motion is denied and after opportunity for hearing, the court shall require the moving party to pay to the party or deponent who opposed the motion the reasonable expenses incurred in opposing the motion that may include attorneys' fees, unless the court finds that the making of the motion was substantially justified or that other circumstances make an award of expenses unjust. If the motion is granted in part and denied in part, the court may apportion the reasonable expenses incurred as a result of making the motion among the parties and persons.

(b) **Failure to Comply with Order**.

(1) If, after being ordered to do so by the court, a deponent fails to be sworn or to answer a question or produce documents, the failure may be considered a contempt of the court.

(2) If a party or an officer, director, or managing agent of a party or a person designated under rule 1.310(b)(6) or 1.320(a) to testify on behalf of a party fails to obey an order to provide or permit discovery, including an order made under subdivision (a) of this rule or rule 1.360, the court in which the action is pending may make any of the following orders:

　(A) An order that the matters regarding which the questions were asked or any other designated facts shall be taken to be established for the purposes of the action in accordance with the claim of the party obtaining the order.

　(B) An order refusing to allow the disobedient party to support or oppose designated claims or defenses, or prohibiting that party from introducing designated matters in evidence.

　(C) An order striking out pleadings or parts of them or staying further proceedings until the order is obeyed, or dismissing the action or proceeding or any part of it, or rendering a judgment by default against the disobedient party.

　(D) Instead of any of the foregoing orders or in addition to them, an order treating as a contempt of court the failure to obey any orders except an order to submit to an examination made pursuant to rule 1.360(a)(1)(B) or subdivision (a)(2) of this rule.

　(E) When a party has failed to comply with an order under rule 1.360(a)(1)(B) requiring that party to produce another for examination, the orders listed in paragraphs (A), (B), and (C) of this subdivision, unless the party failing to comply shows the inability to produce the person for examination.

Instead of any of the foregoing orders or in addition to them, the court shall require the party failing to obey the order to pay the reasonable expenses caused by the failure, which may include attorneys' fees, unless the court finds that the failure was substantially justified or that other circumstances make an award of expenses unjust.

(c) **Expenses on Failure to Admit**. If a party fails to admit the genuineness of any document or the truth of any matter as requested under rule 1.370 and if the party requesting the admissions thereafter proves the genuineness of the document or the truth of the matter, the requesting party may file a motion for an order requiring the other party to pay the requesting party the reasonable expenses incurred in making that proof, which may include attorneys' fees. The court shall issue such an order at the time a party requesting the admissions proves the genuineness of the document or the truth of the matter, upon motion by the requesting party, unless it finds that (1) the request was held objectionable pursuant to rule 1.370(a), (2) the admission sought was of no substantial importance, or (3) there was other good reason for the failure to admit.

(d) **Failure of Party to Attend at Own Deposition or Serve Answers to Interrogatories or Respond to Request for Inspection**. If a party or an officer, director, or managing agent of a party or a person designated under rule 1.310(b)(6) or 1.320(a) to testify on behalf of a party fails (1) to appear before the officer who is to take the deposition after being served with a proper notice, (2) to serve answers or objections to interrogatories submitted under rule 1.340 after proper service of the interrogatories, or (3) to serve a written response to a request for inspection submitted under rule 1.350 after proper service of the request, the court in which the action is pending may take any action authorized under paragraphs (A), (B), and (C) of subdivision (b)(2) of this rule. Any motion specifying a failure under clause (2) or (3) of this subdivision shall include a certification that the movant, in good faith, has conferred or attempted to confer with the party failing to answer or respond in an effort to obtain such answer or response without court action. Instead of any order or in addition to it, the court shall require the party failing to act to pay the reasonable expenses caused by the failure, which may include attorneys' fees, unless the court finds that the failure was substantially justified or that other circumstances make an award of expenses unjust. The failure to act described in this subdivision may not be excused on the ground that the discovery sought is objectionable unless the party failing to act has applied for a protective order as provided by rule 1.280(c).

(e) **Failure to Preserve Electronically Stored Information; Sanctions for Failure to Preserve**. If electronically stored information that should have been preserved in the anticipation or conduct of litigation is lost because a party failed to take reasonable steps to preserve it, and it cannot be restored or replaced through additional discovery, the court:

  (1) upon finding prejudice to another party from loss of the information, may order measures no greater than necessary to cure the prejudice; or

  (2) only upon finding that the party acted with the intent to deprive another party of the information's use in the litigation may:

   (A) presume that the lost information was unfavorable to the party;

   (B) instruct the jury that it may or must presume the information was unfavorable to the party; or

   (C) dismiss the action or enter a default judgment.

Rule 1.390 Depositions of Expert Witnesses

(a) **Definition**. The term "expert witness" as used herein applies exclusively to a person duly and regularly engaged in the practice of a profession who holds a professional degree from a university or college and has had special professional training and experience, or one possessed of special knowledge or skill about the subject upon which called to testify.

(b) **Procedure**. The testimony of an expert or skilled witness may be taken at any time before the trial in accordance with the rules for taking depositions and may be used at trial, regardless of the place of residence of the witness or whether the witness is within the distance prescribed by rule 1.330(a)(3). No special form of notice need be given that the deposition will be used for trial.

(c) **Fee**. An expert or skilled witness whose deposition is taken shall be allowed a witness fee in such reasonable amount as the court may determine. The court shall also determine a reasonable time within which payment must be made, if the deponent and party cannot agree. All parties and the deponent shall be served with notice of any hearing to determine the fee. Any reasonable fee paid to an expert or skilled witness may be taxed as costs.

(d) **Applicability**. Nothing in this rule shall prevent the taking of any deposition as otherwise provided by law.

Rule 1.410 Subpoena

(a) **Subpoena Generally**. Subpoenas for testimony before the court, subpoenas for production of tangible evidence, and subpoenas for taking depositions may be issued by the clerk of court or by any attorney of record in an action.

(b) **Subpoena for Testimony before the Court**.

  (1) Every subpoena for testimony before the court must be issued by an attorney of record in an action or by the clerk under the seal of the court and must state the name of the court and the title of the action and must command each person to whom it is directed to attend and give testimony at a time and place specified in it.

  (2) On oral request of an attorney or party and without praecipe, the clerk must issue a subpoena for testimony before the court or a subpoena for the production of documentary evidence before the court signed and sealed but otherwise in blank, both as to the title of the action and the name of the person to whom it is directed, and the subpoena must be filled in before service by the attorney or party.

(c) **For Production of Documentary Evidence**. A subpoena may also command the person to whom it is directed to produce the books, documents, (including electronically stored information), or tangible things designated therein, but the court, on motion made promptly and in any event at or before the time specified in the subpoena for compliance therewith, may (1) quash or modify the subpoena if it is unreasonable and oppressive, or (2) condition denial of the motion on the advancement by the person in whose behalf the subpoena is issued of the reasonable cost of producing the books, documents, or tangible things. If a subpoena does not specify a form for producing electronically stored information, the person responding must produce it in a form or forms in which it is ordinarily maintained or in a reasonably usable form or forms. A person responding to a subpoena may object to discovery of electronically stored information from sources that the person identifies as not reasonably accessible because of undue costs or burden. On motion to compel discovery or to quash, the person from whom discovery is sought must show that the information sought or the form requested is not reasonably accessible because of undue costs or burden. If that showing is made, the court may nonetheless order discovery from such sources or in such forms if the requesting party shows good cause, considering the limitations set out in rule 1.280(d)(2). The court may specify conditions of the discovery, including ordering that some or all of the expenses of the discovery be paid by the party seeking the discovery. A party seeking production of evidence at trial which would be subject to a subpoena may compel such production by serving a notice to produce such evidence on an adverse party as provided in rule 1.080. Such notice shall have the same effect and be subject to the same limitations as a subpoena served on the party.

(d) **Service**. A subpoena may be served by any person authorized by law to serve process or by any other person who is not a party and who is not less than 18 years of age. Service of a subpoena on a person named within must be made as provided by law. Proof of such service must be made by affidavit of the person making service except as applicable under rule 1.351(c) for the production of documents and things by a nonparty without deposition, if not served by an officer authorized by law to do so.

(e) **Subpoena for Taking Depositions**.

   (1)   Filing a notice to take a deposition as provided in rule 1.310(b) or 1.320(a) with a certificate of service on it showing service on all parties to the action constitutes an authorization for the issuance of subpoenas for the persons named or described in the notice by the clerk of the court in which the action is pending or by an attorney of record in the action. The subpoena must state the method for recording the testimony. The subpoena may command the person to whom it is directed to produce designated books, documents, or tangible things that constitute or contain evidence relating to any of the matters within the scope of the examination permitted by rule 1.280(b), but in that event the subpoena will be subject to the provisions of rule 1.280(c) and subdivision (c) of this rule. Within 10 days after its service, or on or before the time specified in the subpoena for compliance if the time is less than 10 days after service, the person to whom the subpoena is directed may serve written objection to inspection or copying of any of the designated materials. If objection is made, the party serving the subpoena shall not be entitled to inspect and copy the materials except pursuant to an order of the court from which the subpoena was issued. If objection has been made, the party serving the subpoena may move for an order at any time before or during the taking of the deposition on notice to the deponent.

   (2)   A person may be required to attend an examination only in the county wherein the person resides or is employed or transacts business in person or at such other convenient place as may be fixed by an order of court.

(f) **Contempt**. Failure by any person without adequate excuse to obey a subpoena served on that person may be deemed a contempt of the court from which the subpoena issued.

(g) **Depositions before Commissioners Appointed in this State by Courts of Other States; Subpoena Powers; etc**. When any person authorized by the laws of Florida to administer oaths is appointed by a court of record of any other state, jurisdiction, or government as commissioner to take the testimony of any named witness within this state, that witness may be compelled to attend and testify before that commissioner by witness subpoena issued by the clerk of any circuit court at the instance of that commissioner or by other process or proceedings in the same manner as if that commissioner had been appointed by a court of this state; provided that no document shall be compulsorily annexed as an exhibit to such deposition or otherwise permanently removed from the possession of the witness producing it, but in lieu thereof a photostatic copy may be annexed to and transmitted with such executed commission to the court of issuance.

(h) **Subpoena of Minor**. Any minor subpoenaed for testimony has the right to be accompanied by a parent or guardian at all times during the taking of testimony notwithstanding the invocation of the rule of sequestration of section 90.616, Florida Statutes, except on a showing that the presence of a parent or guardian is likely to have a material, negative impact on the credibility or accuracy of the minor's testimony, or that the interests of the parent or guardian are in actual or potential conflict with the interests of the minor.

Rule 1.420 Dismissal of Actions

(a) **Voluntary Dismissal**.

    (1) *By Parties*. Except in actions in which property has been seized or is in the custody of the court, an action, a claim, or any part of an action or claim may be dismissed by plaintiff without order of court (A) before trial by serving, or during trial by stating on the record, a notice of dismissal at any time before a hearing on motion for summary judgment, or if none is served or if the motion is denied, before retirement of the jury in a case tried before a jury or before submission of a nonjury case to the court for decision, or (B) by filing a stipulation of dismissal signed by all current parties to the action. Unless otherwise stated in the notice or stipulation, the dismissal is without prejudice, except that a notice of dismissal operates as an adjudication on the merits when served by a plaintiff who has once dismissed in any court an action based on or including the same claim.

    (2) *By Order of Court; If Counterclaim*. Except as provided in subdivision (a)(1) of this rule, an action shall not be dismissed at a party's instance except on order of the court and upon such terms and conditions as the court deems proper. If a counterclaim has been served by a defendant prior to the service upon the defendant of the plaintiff's notice of dismissal, the action shall not be dismissed against defendant's objections unless the counterclaim can remain pending for independent adjudication by the court. Unless otherwise specified in the order, a dismissal under this paragraph is without prejudice.

(b) **Involuntary Dismissal**. Any party may move for dismissal of an action or of any claim against that party for failure of an adverse party to comply with these rules or any order of court. Notice of hearing on the motion shall be served as required under rule 1.090(d). After a party seeking affirmative relief in an action tried by the court without a jury has completed the presentation of evidence, any other party may move for a dismissal on the ground that on the facts and the law the party seeking affirmative relief has shown no right to relief, without waiving the right to offer evidence if the motion is not granted. The court as trier of the facts may then determine them and render judgment against the party seeking affirmative relief or may decline to render judgment until the close of all the evidence. Unless the court in its order for dismissal otherwise specifies, a dismissal under this subdivision and any dismissal not provided for in this rule, other than a dismissal for lack of jurisdiction or for improper venue or for lack of an indispensable party, operates as an adjudication on the merits.

(c) **Dismissal of Counterclaim, Crossclaim, or Third-Party Claim**. The provisions of this rule apply to the dismissal of any counterclaim, crossclaim, or third-party claim.

(d) **Costs**. Costs in any action dismissed under this rule shall be assessed and judgment for costs entered in that action, once the action is concluded as to the party seeking taxation of costs. When one or more other claims remain pending following dismissal of any claim under this rule, taxable costs attributable solely to the dismissed claim may be assessed and judgment for costs in that claim entered in the action, but only when all claims are resolved at the trial court level as to the party seeking taxation of costs. If a party who has once dismissed a claim in any court of this state commences an action based upon or including the same claim against the same adverse party, the court shall make such order for the payment of costs of the claim previously dismissed as it may deem proper and shall stay the proceedings in the action until the party seeking affirmative relief has complied with the order.

(e) **Failure to Prosecute**. In all actions in which it appears on the face of the record that no activity by filing of pleadings, order of court, or otherwise has occurred for a period of 10 months, and no order staying the action has been issued nor stipulation for stay approved by the court, any interested person, whether a party to the action or not, the court, or the clerk of the court may serve notice to all parties that no such activity has occurred. If no such record activity has occurred within the 10 months immediately preceding the service of such notice, and no record activity occurs within the 60 days immediately following the service of such notice, and if no stay was issued or approved prior to the expiration of such 60-day period, the action shall be dismissed by the court on its own motion or on the motion of any interested person, whether a party to the action or not, after reasonable notice to the parties, unless a party shows good cause in writing at least 5 days before the hearing on the motion why the action should remain pending. Mere inaction for a period of less than 1 year shall not be sufficient cause for dismissal for failure to prosecute.

(f) **Effect on Lis Pendens**. If a notice of lis pendens has been filed in connection with a claim for affirmative relief that is dismissed under this rule, the notice of lis pendens connected with the dismissed claim is automatically dissolved at the same time. The notice, stipulation, or order shall be recorded.

Rule 1.430 Demand for Jury Trial; Waiver

(a) **Right Preserved**. The right of trial by jury as declared by the Constitution or by statute shall be preserved to the parties inviolate.

(b) **Demand**. Any party may demand a trial by jury of any issue triable of right by a jury by serving upon the other party a demand therefor in writing at any time after commencement of the action and not later than 10 days after the service of the last pleading directed to such issue. The demand may be indorsed upon a pleading of the party.

(c) **Specification of Issues**. In the demand a party may specify the issues that the party wishes so tried; otherwise, the party is deemed to demand trial by jury for all issues so triable. If a party has demanded trial by jury for only some of the issues, any other party may serve a demand for trial by jury of any other or all of the issues triable by jury 10 days after service of the demand or such lesser time as the court may order.

(d) **Waiver**. A party who fails to serve a demand as required by this rule waives trial by jury. If waived, a jury trial may not be granted without the consent of the parties, but the court may allow an amendment in the proceedings to demand a trial by jury or order a trial by jury on its own motion. A demand for trial by jury may not be withdrawn without the consent of the parties.

Rule 1.431 Trial Jury

(a) **Questionnaire**.

  (1) The circuit court may direct the authority charged by law with the selection of prospective jurors to furnish each prospective juror with a questionnaire in the form approved by the supreme court from time to time to assist the authority in selecting prospective jurors. The questionnaire must be used after the names of jurors have been selected as provided by law but before certification and the placing of the names of prospective jurors in the jury box. The questionnaire must be used to determine those who are not qualified to serve as jurors under any statutory ground of disqualification.

  (2) To assist in voir dire examination at trial, any court may direct the clerk to furnish prospective jurors selected for service with a questionnaire in the form approved by the supreme court from time to time. The prospective jurors must be asked to complete and return the forms. Completed forms may be inspected in the clerk's office and copies must be available in court during the voir dire examination for use by parties and the court.

(b) **Examination by Parties**. The parties have the right to examine jurors orally on their voir dire. The order in which the parties may examine each juror must be determined by the court. The court may ask such questions of the jurors as it deems necessary, but the right of the parties to conduct a reasonable examination of each juror orally must be preserved.

(c) **Challenge for Cause**.

  (1) On motion of any party, the court must examine any prospective juror on oath to determine whether that person is related, within the third degree, to (i) any party, (ii) the attorney of any party, or (iii) any other person or entity against whom liability or blame is alleged in the pleadings, or is related to any person alleged to have been wronged or injured by the commission of the wrong for the trial of which the juror is called, or has any interest in the action, or has formed or expressed any opinion, or is sensible of any bias or prejudice concerning it, or is an employee or has been an

employee of any party or any other person or entity against whom liability or blame is alleged in the pleadings, within 30 days before the trial. A party objecting to the juror may introduce any other competent evidence to support the objection. If it appears that the juror does not stand indifferent to the action or any of the foregoing grounds of objection exists or that the juror is otherwise incompetent, another must be called in that juror's place.

(2) The fact that any person selected for jury duty from bystanders or the body of the county and not from a jury list lawfully selected has served as a juror in the court in which that person is called at any other time within 1 year is a ground of challenge for cause.

(3) When the nature of any civil action requires a knowledge of reading, writing, and arithmetic, or any of them, to enable a juror to understand the evidence to be offered, the fact that any prospective juror does not possess the qualifications is a ground of challenge for cause.

(d) **Peremptory Challenges**. Each party is entitled to 3 peremptory challenges of jurors, but when the number of parties on opposite sides is unequal, the opposing parties are entitled to the same aggregate number of peremptory challenges to be determined on the basis of 3 peremptory challenges to each party on the side with the greater number of parties. The additional peremptory challenges accruing to multiple parties on the opposing side must be divided equally among them. Any additional peremptory challenges not capable of equal division must be exercised separately or jointly as determined by the court.

(e) **Exercise of Challenges**. All challenges must be addressed to the court outside the hearing of the jury in a manner selected by the court so that the jury panel is not aware of the nature of the challenge, the party making the challenge, or the basis of the court's ruling on the challenge, if for cause.

(f) **Swearing of Jurors**. No one shall be sworn as a juror until the jury has been accepted by the parties or until all challenges have been exhausted.

(g) **Alternate Jurors**.

(1) The court may direct that 1 or more jurors be impaneled to sit as alternate jurors in addition to the regular panel. Alternate jurors in the order in which they are called must replace jurors who have become unable or disqualified to perform their duties before the jury retires to consider its verdict. Alternate jurors must be drawn in the same manner, have the same qualifications, be subject to the same examination, take the same oath, and have the same functions, powers, facilities, and privileges as principal jurors. An alternate juror who does not replace a principal juror must be discharged when the jury retires to consider the verdict.

(2) If alternate jurors are called, each party is entitled to one peremptory challenge in the selection of the alternate juror or jurors, but when the number of parties on opposite sides is unequal, the opposing parties are entitled to the same aggregate number of peremptory challenges to be determined on the basis of 1 peremptory challenge to each party on the side with the greater number of parties. The additional peremptory challenges allowed pursuant to this subdivision may be used only against the alternate jurors. The peremptory challenges allowed pursuant to subdivision (d) of this rule must not be used against the alternate jurors.

(h) **Interview of a Juror**. A party who believes that grounds for legal challenge to a verdict exist may move for an order permitting an interview of a juror or jurors to determine whether the verdict is subject to the challenge. The motion must be served within 15 days after rendition of the verdict unless good cause is shown for the failure to make the motion within that time. The motion must state the name and address of each juror to be interviewed and the grounds for challenge that the party believes may exist. After notice and hearing, the trial judge must enter an order denying the motion or permitting the interview. If the interview is permitted, the court may prescribe the place, manner, conditions, and scope of the interview.

(i) **Communication with the Jury**. This rule governs all communication between the judge or courtroom personnel and jurors.

(1) *Communication to be on the Record.* The court must notify the parties of any communication from the jury pertaining to the action as promptly as practicable and in any event before responding to the communication. Except as set forth below, all communications between the court or courtroom personnel and the jury must be on the record in open court or must be in writing and filed in the action. The court or courtroom personnel must note on any written communication to or from the jury the date and time it was delivered.

(2) *Exception for Certain Routine Communication.* The court must, by pretrial order or by statement on the record with opportunity for objection, set forth the scope of routine ex parte communication to be permitted and the limits imposed by the court with regard to such communication.
   (A) Routine ex parte communication between the bailiff or other courtroom personnel and the jurors, limited to juror comfort and safety, may occur off the record.
   (B) In no event shall ex parte communication between courtroom personnel and jurors extend to matters that may affect the outcome of the trial, including statements containing any fact or opinion concerning a party, attorney, or procedural matter or relating to any legal issue or lawsuit.
(3) *Instructions to Jury.* During voir dire, the court must instruct the jurors and courtroom personnel regarding the limitations on communication between the court or courtroom personnel and jurors. On empanelling the jury, the court must instruct the jurors that their questions are to be submitted in writing to the court, which will review them with the parties and counsel before responding.
(4) *Notification of Jury Communication.* Courtroom personnel must immediately notify the court of any communication to or from a juror or among jurors in contravention of the court's orders or instructions, including all communication contrary to the requirements of this rule.

Rule 1.440 Setting Action for Trial

(a) **When at Issue**. An action is at issue after any motions directed to the last pleading served have been disposed of or, if no such motions are served, 20 days after service of the last pleading. The party entitled to serve motions directed to the last pleading may waive the right to do so by filing a notice for trial at any time after the last pleading is served. The existence of crossclaims among the parties shall not prevent the court from setting the action for trial on the issues raised by the complaint, answer, and any answer to a counterclaim.
(b) **Notice for Trial**. Thereafter any party may file and serve a notice that the action is at issue and ready to be set for trial. The notice shall include an estimate of the time required, whether the trial is to be by a jury or not, and whether the trial is on the original action or a subsequent proceeding. The clerk shall then submit the notice and the case file to the court.
(c) **Setting for Trial**. If the court finds the action ready to be set for trial, it shall enter an order fixing a date for trial. Trial shall be set not less than 30 days from the service of the notice for trial. By giving the same notice the court may set an action for trial. In actions in which the damages are not liquidated, the order setting an action for trial shall be served on parties who are in default in accordance with Florida Rule of General Practice and Judicial Administration 2.516.
(d) **Applicability**. This rule does not apply to actions to which chapter 51, Florida Statutes (1967), applies or to cases designated as complex pursuant to rule 1.201.

Rule 1.442 Proposals for Settlement

(a) **Applicability**. This rule applies to all proposals for settlement authorized by Florida law, regardless of the terms used to refer to such offers, demands, or proposals, and supersedes all other provisions of the rules and statutes that may be inconsistent with this rule.
(b) **Service of Proposal**. A proposal to a defendant shall be served no earlier than 90 days after service of process on that defendant; a proposal to a plaintiff shall be served no earlier than 90 days after the action has been commenced. No proposal shall be served later than 45 days before the date set for trial or the first day of the docket on which the case is set for trial, whichever is earlier.
(c) **Form and Content of Proposal for Settlement**.
   (1) A proposal shall be in writing and shall identify the applicable Florida law under which it is being made.
   (2) A proposal shall:
      (A) name the party or parties making the proposal and the party or parties to whom the proposal is being made;
      (B) state that the proposal resolves all damages that would otherwise be awarded in a final judgment in the action in which the proposal is served, subject to subdivision (F);
      (C) state with particularity any relevant conditions;

       (D) state the total amount of the proposal and state with particularity all nonmonetary terms of the proposal;

       (E) state with particularity the amount proposed to settle a claim for punitive damages, if any;

       (F) state whether the proposal includes attorneys' fees and whether attorneys' fee are part of the legal claim; and

       (G) include a certificate of service in the form required by Florida Rule of General Practice and Judicial Administration 2.516.

   (3) A proposal may be made by or to any party or parties and by or to any combination of parties properly identified in the proposal. A joint proposal shall state the amount and terms attributable to each party.

   (4) Notwithstanding subdivision (c)(3), when a party is alleged to be solely vicariously, constructively, derivatively, or technically liable, whether by operation of law or by contract, a joint proposal made by or served on such a party need not state the apportionment or contribution as to that party. Acceptance by any party shall be without prejudice to rights of contribution or indemnity.

(d) **Service and Filing**. A proposal shall be served on the party or parties to whom it is made but shall not be filed unless necessary to enforce the provisions of this rule.

(e) **Withdrawal**. A proposal may be withdrawn in writing provided the written withdrawal is delivered before a written acceptance is delivered. Once withdrawn, a proposal is void.

(f) **Acceptance and Rejection**.

   (1) A proposal shall be deemed rejected unless accepted by delivery of a written notice of acceptance within 30 days after service of the proposal. The provisions of Florida Rule of General Practice and Judicial Administration 2.514(b) do not apply to this subdivision. No oral communications shall constitute an acceptance, rejection, or counteroffer under the provisions of this rule.

   (2) In any case in which the existence of a class is alleged, the time for acceptance of a proposal for settlement is extended to 30 days after the date the order granting or denying certification is filed.

(g) **Sanctions**. Any party seeking sanctions pursuant to applicable Florida law, based on the failure of the proposal's recipient to accept a proposal, shall do so by serving a motion in accordance with rule 1.525.

(h) **Costs and Fees**.

   (1) If a party is entitled to costs and fees pursuant to applicable Florida law, the court may, in its discretion, determine that a proposal was not made in good faith. In such case, the court may disallow an award of costs and attorneys' fees.

   (2) When determining the reasonableness of the amount of an award of attorneys' fees pursuant to this section, the court shall consider, along with all other relevant criteria, the following factors:

       (A) The then-apparent merit or lack of merit in the claim.

       (B) The number and nature of proposals made by the parties.

       (C) The closeness of questions of fact and law at issue.

       (D) Whether the party making the proposal had unreasonably refused to furnish information necessary to evaluate the reasonableness of the proposal.

       (E) Whether the suit was in the nature of a test case presenting questions of far-reaching importance affecting nonparties.

       (F) The amount of the additional delay cost and expense that the party making the proposal reasonably would be expected to incur if the litigation were to be prolonged.

(i) **Evidence of Proposal**. Evidence of a proposal or acceptance thereof is admissible only in proceedings to enforce an accepted proposal or to determine the imposition of sanctions.

(j) **Effect of Mediation**. Mediation shall have no effect on the dates during which parties are permitted to make or accept a proposal for settlement under the terms of the rule.

Rule 1.450 Evidence

(a) **Record of Excluded Evidence**. In an action tried by a jury if an objection to a question propounded to a witness is sustained by the court, the examining attorney may make a specific offer of what the attorney expects to prove by the answer of the witness. The court may require the offer to be made out of the hearing of the jury. The court may add such other or further statement as clearly shows the character of the evidence, the form in which it was offered, the objection made, and the ruling thereon. In actions tried without a jury the same procedure may be followed except that the court upon request shall take and report the evidence in full unless it clearly appears that the evidence is not admissible on any ground or that the witness is privileged.

(b) **Filing**. When documentary evidence is introduced in an action, the clerk or the judge shall endorse an identifying number or symbol on it and when proffered or admitted in evidence, it shall be filed by the clerk or judge and considered in the custody of the court and not withdrawn except with written leave of court.

Rule 1.451 Taking Testimony

(a) **Testimony at Hearing or Trial**. When testifying at a hearing or trial, a witness must be physically present unless otherwise provided by law or rule of procedure.

(b) **Communication Equipment**. The court may permit a witness to testify at a hearing or trial by contemporaneous audio or video communication equipment (1) by agreement of the parties or (2) for good cause shown upon written request of a party upon reasonable notice to all other parties. The request and notice must contain the substance of the proposed testimony and an estimate of the length of the proposed testimony. In considering sufficient good cause, the court shall weigh and address in its order the reasons stated for testimony by communication equipment against the potential for prejudice to the objecting party.

(c) **Required Equipment**. Communication equipment as used in this rule means a conference telephone or other electronic device that permits all those appearing or participating to hear and speak to each other simultaneously and permits all conversations of all parties to be audible to all persons present. Contemporaneous video communications equipment must make the witness visible to all participants during the testimony. For testimony by any of the foregoing means, there must be appropriate safeguards for the court to maintain sufficient control over the equipment and the transmission of the testimony so the court may stop the communication to accommodate objection or prevent prejudice.

(d) **Oath**. Testimony may be taken through communication equipment only if a notary public or other person authorized to administer oaths in the witness's jurisdiction is present with the witness and administers the oath consistent with the laws of the jurisdiction.

(e) **Burden of Expense**. The cost for the use of the communication equipment is the responsibility of the requesting party unless otherwise ordered by the court.

Rule 1.452 Questions by Jurors

(a) **Questions Permitted**. The court shall permit jurors to submit to the court written questions directed to witnesses or to the court. Such questions will be submitted after all counsel have concluded their questioning of a witness.

(b) **Procedure**. Any juror who has a question directed to the witness or the court shall prepare an unsigned, written question and give the question to the bailiff, who will give the question to the judge.

(c) **Objections**. Out of the presence of the jury, the judge will read the question to all counsel, allow counsel to see the written question, and give counsel an opportunity to object to the question.

Rule 1.455 Juror Notebooks

In its discretion, the court may authorize documents and exhibits to be included in notebooks for use by the jurors during trial to aid them in performing their duties.

Rule 1.460 Continuances

A motion for continuance shall be in writing unless made at a trial and, except for good cause shown, shall be signed by the party requesting the continuance. The motion shall state all of the facts that the movant contends entitle the movant to a continuance. If a continuance is sought on the ground of nonavailability of a witness, the motion must show when it is believed the witness will be available.

Rule 1.470 Exceptions Unnecessary; Jury Instructions

(a) **Adverse Ruling**. For appellate purposes no exception shall be necessary to any adverse ruling, order, instruction, or thing whatsoever said or done at the trial or prior thereto or after verdict, which was said or done after objection made and considered by the trial court and which affected the substantial rights of the party complaining and which is assigned as error.

(b) **Instructions to Jury**. The Florida Standard Jury Instructions appearing on The Florida Bar's website may be used, as provided in Florida Rule of General Practice and Judicial Administration 2.570, by the trial judges in instructing the jury in civil actions. Not later than at the close of the evidence, the parties shall file written requests that the court instruct the jury on the law set forth in such requests. The court shall then require counsel to appear before it to settle the instructions to be given. At such conference, all objections shall be made and ruled upon and the court shall inform counsel of such instructions as it will give. No party may assign as error the giving of any instruction unless that party objects thereto at such time, or the failure to give any instruction unless that party requested the same. The court shall orally instruct the jury before or after the arguments of counsel and may provide appropriate instructions during the trial. If the instructions are given prior to final argument, the presiding judge shall give the jury final procedural instructions after final arguments are concluded and prior to deliberations. The court shall provide each juror with a written set of the instructions for his or her use in deliberations. The court shall file a copy of such instructions.

(c) **Orders on New Trial, Directed Verdicts, etc**. It shall not be necessary to object or except to any order granting or denying motions for new trials, directed verdicts, or judgments non obstante veredicto or in arrest of judgment to entitle the party against whom such ruling is made to have the same reviewed by an appellate court.

Rule 1.480 Motion for a Directed Verdict

(a) **Effect**. A party who moves for a directed verdict at the close of the evidence offered by the adverse party may offer evidence in the event the motion is denied without having reserved the right to do so and to the same extent as if the motion had not been made. The denial of a motion for a directed verdict shall not operate to discharge the jury. A motion for a directed verdict shall state the specific grounds therefor. The order directing a verdict is effective without any assent of the jury.

(b) **Reservation of Decision on Motion**. When a motion for a directed verdict is denied or for any reason is not granted, the court is deemed to have submitted the action to the jury subject to a later determination of the legal questions raised by the motion. Within 15 days after the return of a verdict, a party who has timely moved for a directed verdict may serve a motion to set aside the verdict and any judgment entered thereon and to enter judgment in accordance with the motion for a directed verdict. If a verdict was not returned, a party who has timely moved for a directed verdict may serve a motion for judgment in accordance with the motion for a directed verdict within 15 days after discharge of the jury.

(c) **Joined with Motion for New Trial**. A motion for a new trial may be joined with this motion or a new trial may be requested in the alternative. If a verdict was returned, the court may allow the judgment to stand or may reopen the judgment and either order a new trial or direct the entry of judgment as if the requested verdict had been directed. If no verdict was returned, the court may direct the entry of judgment as if the requested verdict had been directed or may order a new trial.

Rule 1.481 Verdicts

In all actions when punitive damages are sought, the verdict shall state the amount of punitive damages separately from the amounts of other damages awarded.

Rule 1.490 Magistrates

(a) **General Magistrates**. Judges of the circuit court may appoint as many general magistrates from among the members of the Bar in the circuit as the judges find necessary, and the general magistrates shall continue in office until removed by the court. The order making an appointment shall be recorded. Every person appointed as a general magistrate shall take the oath required of officers by the Constitution and the oath shall be recorded before the magistrate discharges any duties of that office.

(b) **Special Magistrates**. The court may appoint members of The Florida Bar as special magistrates for any particular service required by the court, and they shall be governed by all the provisions of law and rules relating to magistrates except they shall not be required to make oath or give bond unless specifically required by the order appointing them. Upon a showing that the appointment is advisable, a person other than a member of the Bar may be appointed.

(c) **Reference**. No reference shall be to a magistrate, either general or special, without the consent of the parties. When a reference is made to a magistrate, either party may set the action for hearing before the magistrate.

(d) **General Powers and Duties**. Every magistrate shall perform all of the duties that pertain to the office according to the practice in chancery and under the direction of the court. Process issued by a magistrate shall be directed as provided by law. Hearings before any magistrate, examiner, or commissioner shall be held in the county where the action is pending, but hearings may be held at any place by order of the court within or without the state to meet the convenience of the witnesses or the parties. All grounds of disqualification of a judge shall apply to magistrates. Magistrates shall not practice law of the same case type in the court or circuit the magistrate is appointed to serve.

(e) **Bond**. When not otherwise provided by law, the court may require magistrates who are appointed to dispose of real or personal property to give bond and surety conditioned for the proper payment of all moneys that may come into their hands and for the due performance of their duties as the court may direct. The bond shall be made payable to the State of Florida and shall be for the benefit of all persons aggrieved by any act of the magistrate.

(f) **Notice of Hearings**. The magistrate shall assign a time and place for proceedings as soon as reasonably possible after the reference is made and give notice to each of the parties. The notice or order setting a matter for hearing before the magistrate must state if electronic recording or a court reporter will be used to create a record of the proceedings. If electronic recording is to be used, the notice must state that any party may have a court reporter transcribe the record of the proceedings at that party's expense. If any party fails to appear, the magistrate may proceed ex parte or may adjourn the proceeding to a future day, giving notice to the absent party of the adjournment.

(g) **Hearings**. The magistrate shall proceed with reasonable diligence in every reference and with the least practicable delay. Any party may apply to the court for an order to the magistrate to speed the proceedings and to make the report and to certify to the court the reason for any delay. The evidence shall be taken by the magistrate or by some other person under the magistrate's authority in the magistrate's presence and shall be filed with the magistrate's report. The magistrate shall have authority to examine on oath the parties and all witnesses produced by the parties on all matters contained in the reference and to require production of all books, papers, writings, vouchers, and other documents applicable to the referenced matters. The magistrate shall admit evidence by deposition or that is otherwise admissible in court. The magistrate may take all actions concerning evidence that can be taken by the court and in the same manner. All parties accounting before a magistrate shall bring in their accounts in the form of accounts payable and receivable, and any other parties who are not satisfied with the account may examine the accounting party orally or by interrogatories or deposition as the magistrate directs. All depositions and documents that have been taken or used previously in the action may be used before the magistrate.

(h) **Magistrate's Report**. The magistrate must file the report on the referenced matters and served copies on all parties, and include the name and address of any court reporter who transcribed the proceedings. The magistrate's report must contain the following language in bold type: IF YOU WISH TO SEEK REVIEW OF THE REPORT AND RECOMMENDATIONS MADE BY THE MAGISTRATE, YOU MUST FILE EXCEPTIONS IN ACCORDANCE WITH FLORIDA RULE OF CIVIL PROCEDURE 1.490(i). YOU WILL BE REQUIRED TO PROVIDE THE COURT WITH A RECORD SUFFICIENT TO SUPPORT YOUR EXCEPTIONS OR YOUR EXCEPTIONS WILL BE DENIED. A RECORD ORDINARILY INCLUDES A WRITTEN TRANSCRIPT OF ALL RELEVANT PROCEEDINGS. THE PERSON SEEKING REVIEW MUST HAVE THE TRANSCRIPT PREPARED IF NECESSARY FOR THE COURT'S REVIEW.

(i) **Filing Report; Notice; Exceptions**. The parties may file exceptions to the report within 10 days after it is served. Any party may file cross-exceptions within 5 days from the service of the exceptions. If no exceptions are timely filed the court shall take appropriate action on the report. If exceptions are filed, the court shall resolve the exceptions at a hearing on reasonable notice. The filing of cross-exceptions shall not delay a hearing on the exceptions and cross-exceptions unless good cause is shown.

(j) **Record**. A party filing exceptions to the magistrate's report must provide the court in advance of the hearing a record sufficient to support that party's exceptions.

    (1)   The record shall include the court file, designated portions of the transcript of proceedings before the magistrate, and all depositions and evidence presented to the magistrate. The designated transcript portions must be delivered to the court and all other parties at least 48 hours before the hearing.

    (2)   If the party filing exceptions has the court reporter prepare less than a full transcript of proceedings before the magistrate, that party must promptly file a notice designating the portions of the transcript that have been ordered. The other parties must be given reasonable time after service of the notice to arrange for the preparation and designation of other portions of the transcript for the court to consider at the hearing.

Rule 1.491 General Magistrates for Residential Mortgage Foreclosure Matters

(a) **General Magistrates for Residential Mortgage Foreclosure**. The chief judge of each judicial circuit shall appoint such number of general magistrates to handle only residential mortgage foreclosures from among the members of the Bar in the circuit as are necessary to expeditiously preside over all actions and suits for the foreclosure of a mortgage on residential real property; and any other matter concerning the foreclosure of a mortgage on residential real property as allowed by the administrative order of the chief judge. Such general magistrates shall continue in office until removed by the court. The order making an appointment shall be recorded. Every person appointed as a general magistrate shall take the oath required of officers by the Constitution and the oath shall be recorded before the magistrate discharges any duties of that office. General magistrates appointed to handle residential mortgage foreclosure matters only shall not be required to give bond or surety.

(b) **Reference**.

    (1)   Consent to a magistrate for residential mortgage foreclosure actions and suits may be express or may be implied in accordance with the requirements of this rule.

        (A) A written objection to the referral to a magistrate handling residential mortgage foreclosures must be filed within 10 days of the service of the order of referral or within the time to respond to the initial pleading, whichever is later.

        (B) If the time set for the hearing is less than 10 days after service of the order of referral, the objection must be filed before commencement of the hearing.

        (C) Failure to file a written objection to a referral to the magistrate handling residential mortgage foreclosures within the applicable time period is deemed to be consent to the order of referral.

    (2)   The order of referral to a magistrate handling residential mortgage foreclosures shall be in substantial conformity with this rule and shall contain the following language in bold type: A REFERRAL TO A MAGISTRATE FOR A RESIDENTIAL MORTGAGE FORECLOSURE MATTER REQUIRES THE CONSENT OF ALL PARTIES. YOU ARE ENTITLED TO HAVE THIS MATTER HEARD BEFORE A JUDGE. IF YOU DO NOT WANT TO HAVE THIS MATTER HEARD BEFORE A MAGISTRATE, YOU MUST FILE A WRITTEN OBJECTION TO THE REFERRAL WITHIN 10 DAYS OF THE TIME OF SERVICE OF THIS ORDER OR WITHIN THE TIME TO RESPOND TO THE INITIAL PLEADING, WHICHEVER IS LATER. IF THE TIME SET FOR THE HEARING IS LESS THAN 10 DAYS AFTER THE SERVICE OF THIS ORDER, THE OBJECTION MUST BE MADE BEFORE THE HEARING. FAILURE TO FILE A WRITTEN OBJECTION WITHIN THE APPLICABLE TIME PERIOD IS DEEMED TO BE CONSENT TO THE REFERRAL. REVIEW OF THE REPORT AND RECOMMENDATIONS MADE BY THE MAGISTRATE SHALL BE BY EXCEPTIONS AS PROVIDED IN THIS RULE. A RECORD, WHICH INCLUDES A TRANSCRIPT OF PROCEEDINGS, MAY BE REQUIRED TO SUPPORT THE EXCEPTIONS.

When a reference is made to a magistrate, either party may set the action for hearing before the magistrate.

(c) **General Powers and Duties**. The provisions for the general powers and duties of a magistrate in rule 1.490(d) shall apply to proceedings under this rule.

(d) **Notice of Hearings; Hearings**. The provisions for notice of hearings and hearings in rules 1.490(f)-(g) shall apply to proceedings under this rule.

(e) **Magistrate's Report**. The provisions for the requirement of the magistrate's report in rule 1.490(h) shall apply to proceedings under this rule.

(f) **Filing Report; Notice; Exceptions; Record**. The provisions for filing the report, notice, exceptions to the report, and requirements for a record in rules 1.490(i)-(j) shall apply to proceedings under this rule.

Rule 1.500 Defaults and Final Judgments Thereon

(a) **By the Clerk**. When a party against whom affirmative relief is sought has failed to file or serve any document in the action, the party seeking relief may have the clerk enter a default against the party failing to serve or file such document.

(b) **By the Court**. When a party against whom affirmative relief is sought has failed to plead or otherwise defend as provided by these rules or any applicable statute or any order of court, the court may enter a default against such party; provided that if such party has filed or served any document in the action, that party must be served with notice of the application for default.

(c) **Right to Plead**. A party may plead or otherwise defend at any time before default is entered. If a party in default files any document after the default is entered, the clerk must notify the party of the entry of the default. The clerk must make an entry on the progress docket showing the notification.

(d) **Setting aside Default**. The court may set aside a default, and if a final judgment consequent thereon has been entered, the court may set it aside in accordance with rule 1.540(b).

(e) **Final Judgment**. Final judgments after default may be entered by the court at any time, but no judgment may be entered against an infant or incompetent person unless represented in the action by a general guardian, committee, conservator, or other representative who has appeared in it or unless the court has made an order under rule 1.210(b) providing that no representative is necessary for the infant or incompetent. If it is necessary to take an account or to determine the amount of damages or to establish the truth of any averment by evidence or to make an investigation of any other matter to enable the court to enter judgment or to effectuate it, the court may receive affidavits, make references, or conduct hearings as it deems necessary and must accord a right of trial by jury to the parties when required by the Constitution or any statute.

Rule 1.510 Summary Judgment

(a) **Motion for Summary Judgment or Partial Summary Judgment**. A party may move for summary judgment, identifying each claim or defense-or the part of each claim or defense-on which summary judgment is sought. The court shall grant summary judgment if the movant shows that there is no genuine dispute as to any material fact and the movant is entitled to judgment as a matter of law. The court shall state on the record the reasons for granting or denying the motion. The summary judgment standard provided for in this rule shall be construed and applied in accordance with the federal summary judgment standard.

(b) **Time to File a Motion**. A party may move for summary judgment at any time after the expiration of 20 days from the commencement of the action or after service of a motion for summary judgment by the adverse party. The movant must serve the motion for summary judgment at least 40 days before the time fixed for the hearing.

(c) **Procedures**.

(1) *Supporting Factual Positions*. A party asserting that a fact cannot be or is genuinely disputed must support the assertion by:

(A) citing to particular parts of materials in the record, including depositions, documents, electronically stored information, affidavits or declarations, stipulations (including those made for purposes of the motion only), admissions, interrogatory answers, or other materials; or

(B) showing that the materials cited do not establish the absence or presence of a genuine dispute, or that an adverse party cannot produce admissible evidence to support the fact.

(2) *Objection That a Fact Is Not Supported by Admissible Evidence*. A party may object that the material cited to support or dispute a fact cannot be presented in a form that would be admissible in evidence.

(3) *Materials Not Cited*. The court need consider only the cited materials, but it may consider other materials in the record.

(4) *Affidavits or Declarations*. An affidavit or declaration used to support or oppose a motion must be made on personal knowledge, set out facts that would be admissible in evidence, and show that the affiant or declarant is competent to testify on the matters stated.

(5) *Timing for Supporting Factual Positions*. At the time of filing a motion for summary judgment, the movant must also serve the movant's supporting factual position as provided in subdivision (1) above. At least 20 days before the time fixed for the hearing, the nonmovant must serve a response that includes the nonmovant's supporting factual position as provided in subdivision (1) above.

(d) **When Facts Are Unavailable to the Nonmovant**. If a nonmovant shows by affidavit or declaration that, for specified reasons, it cannot present facts essential to justify its opposition, the court may:

    (1) defer considering the motion or deny it;

    (2) allow time to obtain affidavits or declarations or to take discovery; or

    (3) issue any other appropriate order.

(e) **Failing to Properly Support or Address a Fact**. If a party fails to properly support an assertion of fact or fails to properly address another party's assertion of fact as required by rule 1.510(c), the court may:

    (1) give an opportunity to properly support or address the fact;

    (2) consider the fact undisputed for purposes of the motion;

    (3) grant summary judgment if the motion and supporting materials-including the facts considered undisputed-show that the movant is entitled to it; or

    (4) issue any other appropriate order.

(f) **Judgment Independent of the Motion**. After giving notice and a reasonable time to respond, the court may:

    (1) grant summary judgment for a nonmovant;

    (2) grant the motion on grounds not raised by a party; or

    (3) consider summary judgment on its own after identifying for the parties material facts that may not be genuinely in dispute.

(g) **Failing to Grant All the Requested Relief**. If the court does not grant all the relief requested by the motion, it may enter an order stating any material fact-including an item of damages or other relief-that is not genuinely in dispute and treating the fact as established in the case.

(h) **Affidavit or Declaration Submitted in Bad Faith**. If satisfied that an affidavit or declaration under this rule is submitted in bad faith or solely for delay, the court-after notice and a reasonable time to respond-may order the submitting party to pay the other party the reasonable expenses, including attorney's fees, it incurred as a result. An offending party or attorney may also be held in contempt or subjected to other appropriate sanctions.

Rule 1.520 View

Upon motion of either party the jury may be taken to view the premises or place in question or any property, matter, or thing relating to the controversy between the parties when it appears that view is necessary to a just decision; but the party making the motion shall advance a sum sufficient to defray the expenses of the jury and the officer who attends them in taking the view, which expense shall be taxed as costs if the party who advanced it prevails.

Rule 1.525 Motions for Costs and Attorneys' Fees

Any party seeking a judgment taxing costs, attorneys' fees, or both shall serve a motion no later than 30 days after filing of the judgment, including a judgment of dismissal, or the service of a notice of voluntary dismissal, which judgment or notice concludes the action as to that party.

Rule 1.530 Motions for New Trial and Rehearing; Amendments of Judgments

(a) **Jury and Non-Jury Actions**. A new trial may be granted to all or any of the parties and on all or a part of the issues. On a motion for a rehearing of matters heard without a jury, including summary judgments, the court may open the judgment if one has been entered, take additional testimony, and enter a new judgment.

(b) **Time for Motion**. A motion for new trial or for rehearing shall be served not later than 15 days after the return of the verdict in a jury action or the date of filing of the judgment in a non-jury action. A timely motion may be amended to state new grounds in the discretion of the court at any time before the motion is determined.

(c) **Time for Serving Affidavits**. When a motion for a new trial is based on affidavits, the affidavits shall be served with the motion. The opposing party has 10 days after such service within which to serve opposing affidavits, which period may be extended for an additional period not exceeding 20 days either by the court for good cause shown or by the parties by written stipulation. The court may permit reply affidavits.

(d) **On Initiative of Court**. Not later than 15 days after entry of judgment or within the time of ruling on a timely motion for a rehearing or a new trial made by a party, the court of its own initiative may order a rehearing or a new trial for any reason for which it might have granted a rehearing or a new trial on motion of a party.

(e) **When Motion Is Unnecessary; Non-Jury Case**. When an action has been tried by the court without a jury, the sufficiency of the evidence to support the judgment may be raised on appeal whether or not the party raising the question has made any objection thereto in the trial court or made a motion for rehearing, for new trial, or to alter or amend the judgment.

(f) **Order Granting to Specify Grounds**. All orders granting a new trial shall specify the specific grounds therefor. If such an order is appealed and does not state the specific grounds, the appellate court shall relinquish its jurisdiction to the trial court for entry of an order specifying the grounds for granting the new trial.

(g) **Motion to Alter or Amend a Judgment**. A motion to alter or amend the judgment shall be served not later than 15 days after entry of the judgment, except that this rule does not affect the remedies in rule 1.540(b).

Rule 1.535 Remittitur and Additur

(a) Within the time provided in rule 1.530(b), any party may serve a motion for remittitur or additur. The motion shall state the applicable Florida law under which it is being made, the amount the movant contends the verdict should be, and the specific evidence that supports the amount stated or a statement of the improper elements of damages included in the damages award.

(b) If a remittitur or additur is granted, the court must state the specific statutory criteria relied on.

(c) Any party adversely affected by the order granting remittitur or additur may reject the award and elect a new trial on the issue of damages only by filing a written election within 15 days after the order granting remittitur or additur is filed.

Rule 1.540 Relief from Judgment, Decrees, or Orders

(a) **Clerical Mistakes**. Clerical mistakes in judgments, decrees, or other parts of the record and errors therein arising from oversight or omission may be corrected by the court at any time on its own initiative or on the motion of any party and after such notice, if any, as the court orders. During the pendency of an appeal such mistakes may be so corrected before the record on appeal is docketed in the appellate court, and thereafter while the appeal is pending may be so corrected with leave of the appellate court.

(b) **Mistakes; Inadvertence; Excusable Neglect; Newly Discovered Evidence; Fraud; etc**. On motion and upon such terms as are just, the court may relieve a party or a party's legal representative from a final judgment, decree, order, or proceeding for the following reasons:

    (1) mistake, inadvertence, surprise, or excusable neglect;

    (2) newly discovered evidence which by due diligence could not have been discovered in time to move for a new trial or rehearing;

    (3) fraud (whether heretofore denominated intrinsic or extrinsic), misrepresentation, or other misconduct of an adverse party;

    (4) that the judgment, decree, or order is void; or

    (5) that the judgment, decree, or order has been satisfied, released, or discharged, or a prior judgment, decree, or order upon which it is based has been reversed or otherwise vacated, or it is no longer equitable that the judgment, decree, or order should have prospective application.

The motion shall be filed within a reasonable time, and for reasons (1), (2), and (3) not more than 1 year after the judgment, decree, order, or proceeding was entered or taken. A motion under this subdivision does not affect the finality of a judgment, decree, or order or suspend its operation. This rule does not limit the power of a court to entertain an independent action to relieve a party from a judgment, decree, order, or proceeding or to set aside a judgment, decree, or order for fraud upon the court.
Writs of coram nobis, coram vobis, audita querela, and bills of review and bills in the nature of a bill of review are abolished, and the procedure for obtaining any relief from a judgment or decree shall be by motion as prescribed in these rules or by an independent action.

Rule 1.545 Final Disposition Form

A final disposition form (form 1.998) must be filed with the clerk by the prevailing party at the time of the filing of the order or judgment which disposes of the action. If the action is settled without a court order or judgment being entered, or dismissed by the parties, the plaintiff or petitioner immediately must file a final disposition form (form 1.998) with the clerk. The clerk must complete the final disposition form for a party appearing pro se, or when the action is dismissed by court order for lack of prosecution pursuant to rule 1.420(e).

Rule 1.550 Executions and Final Process

(a) **Issuance**. Executions on judgments shall issue during the life of the judgment on the oral request of the party entitled to it or that party's attorney without praecipe. No execution or other final process shall issue until the judgment on which it is based has been recorded nor within the time for serving a motion for new trial or rehearing, and if a motion for new trial or rehearing is timely served, until it is determined; provided execution or other final process may be issued on special order of the court at any time after judgment.

(b) **Stay**. The court before which an execution or other process based on a final judgment is returnable may stay such execution or other process and suspend proceedings thereon for good cause on motion and notice to all adverse parties.

Rule 1.560 Discovery in Aid of Execution

(a) **In General**. In aid of a judgment, decree, or execution the judgment creditor or the successor in interest, when that interest appears of record, may obtain discovery from any person, including the judgment debtor, in the manner provided in these rules.

(b) **Fact Information Sheet**. In addition to any other discovery available to a judgment creditor under this rule, the court, at the request of the judgment creditor, shall order the judgment debtor or debtors to complete form 1.977, including all required attachments, within 45 days of the order or such other reasonable time as determined by the court. Failure to obey the order may be considered contempt of court.

(c) **Final Judgment Enforcement Paragraph**. In any final judgment, the judge shall include the following enforcement paragraph if requested by the prevailing party or attorney: "It is further ordered and adjudged that the judgment debtor(s) shall complete under oath Florida Rule of Civil Procedure Form 1.977 (Fact Information Sheet), including all required attachments, and serve it on the judgment creditor's attorney, or the judgment creditor if the judgment creditor is not represented by an attorney, within 45 days from the date of this final judgment, unless the final judgment is satisfied or post-judgment discovery is stayed.

Jurisdiction of this case is retained to enter further orders that are proper to compel the judgment debtor(s) to complete form 1.977, including all required attachments, and serve it on the judgment creditor's attorney, or the judgment creditor if the judgment creditor is not represented by an attorney."

(d) **Information Regarding Assets of Judgment Debtor's Spouse**. In any final judgment, if requested by the judgment creditor, the court shall include the additional Spouse Related Portion of the fact information sheet upon a showing that a proper predicate exists for discovery of separate income and assets of the judgment debtor's spouse.

Rule 1.570 Enforcement of Final Judgments

(a) **Money Judgments**. Final process to enforce a judgment solely for the payment of money shall be by execution, writ of garnishment, or other appropriate process or proceedings.

(b) **Property Recovery**. Final process to enforce a judgment for the recovery of property shall be by a writ of possession for real property and by a writ of replevin, distress writ, writ of garnishment, or other appropriate process or proceedings for other property.

(c) **Performance of an Act**. If judgment is for the performance of a specific act or contract:

    (1) the judgment shall specify the time within which the act shall be performed. If the act is not performed within the time specified, the party seeking enforcement of the judgment shall make an affidavit that the judgment has not been complied with within the prescribed time and the clerk shall issue a writ of attachment against the delinquent party. The delinquent party shall not be released from the writ of attachment until that party has complied with the judgment and paid all costs accruing because of the failure to perform the act. If the delinquent party cannot be found, the party seeking enforcement of the judgment shall file an affidavit to this effect and the court shall issue a writ of sequestration against the delinquent party's property. The writ of sequestration shall not be dissolved until the delinquent party complies with the judgment;

    (2) the court may hold the disobedient party in contempt; or

    (3) the court may appoint some person, not a party to the action, to perform the act insofar as practicable. The performance of the act by the person appointed shall have the same effect as if performed by the party against whom the judgment was entered.

(d) **Vesting Title**. If the judgment is for a conveyance, transfer, release, or acquittance of real or personal property, the judgment shall have the effect of a duly executed conveyance, transfer, release, or acquittance that is recorded in the county where the judgment is recorded. A judgment under this subdivision shall be effective notwithstanding any disability of a party.

(e) **Proceedings Supplementary**. Proceedings supplementary to execution and related discovery shall proceed as provided by chapter 56, Florida Statutes. Notices to Appear, as defined by law, and supplemental complaints in proceedings supplementary must be served as provided by the law and rules of procedure for service of process.

Rule 1.580 Writ of Possession

(a) **Issuance**. When a judgment or order is for the delivery of possession of real property, the judgment or order shall direct the clerk to issue a writ of possession. The clerk shall issue the writ forthwith and deliver it to the sheriff for execution.

(b) **Third-Party Claims**. If a person other than the party against whom the writ of possession is issued is in possession of the property, that person may retain possession of the property by filing with the sheriff an affidavit that the person is entitled to possession of the property, specifying the nature of the claim. Thereupon the sheriff shall desist from enforcing the writ and shall serve a copy of the affidavit on the party causing issuance of the writ of possession. The party causing issuance of the writ may apply to the court for an order directing the sheriff to complete execution of the writ. The court shall determine the right of possession in the property and shall order the sheriff to continue to execute the writ or shall stay execution of the writ, if appropriate.

Rule 1.590 Process in Behalf of and Against Persons Not Parties

Every person who is not a party to the action who has obtained an order, or in whose favor an order has been made, may enforce obedience to such order by the same process as if that person were a party, and every person, not a party, against whom obedience to any order may be enforced shall be liable to the same process for enforcing obedience to such orders as if that person were a party.

Rule 1.600 Deposits in Court

In an action in which any part of the relief sought is a judgment for a sum of money or the disposition of a sum of money or the disposition of any other thing capable of delivery, a party may deposit all or any part of such sum or thing with the court upon notice to every other party and by leave of court. Money paid into court under this rule shall be deposited and withdrawn by order of court.

Rule 1.610 Injunctions

(a) **Temporary Injunction**.
  (1) A temporary injunction may be granted without written or oral notice to the adverse party only if:
    (A) it appears from the specific facts shown by affidavit or verified pleading that immediate and irreparable injury, loss, or damage will result to the movant before the adverse party can be heard in opposition; and
    (B) the movant's attorney certifies in writing any efforts that have been made to give notice and the reasons why notice should not be required.
  (2) No evidence other than the affidavit or verified pleading shall be used to support the application for a temporary injunction unless the adverse party appears at the hearing or has received reasonable notice of the hearing. Every temporary injunction granted without notice shall be endorsed with the date and hour of entry and shall be filed forthwith in the clerk's office and shall define the injury, state findings by the court why the injury may be irreparable, and give the reasons why the order was granted without notice if notice was not given. The temporary injunction shall remain in effect until the further order of the court.

(b) **Bond**. No temporary injunction shall be entered unless a bond is given by the movant in an amount the court deems proper, conditioned for the payment of costs and damages sustained by the adverse party if the adverse party is wrongfully enjoined. Unless otherwise specified by the court, the bond shall be posted within 5 days of entry of the order setting the bond. When any injunction is issued on the pleading of a municipality or the state or any officer, agency, or political subdivision thereof, the court may require or dispense with a bond, with or without surety, and conditioned in the same manner, having due regard for the public interest. No bond shall be required for issuance of a temporary injunction issued solely to prevent physical injury or abuse of a natural person.

(c) **Form and Scope**. Every injunction shall specify the reasons for entry, shall describe in reasonable detail the act or acts restrained without reference to a pleading or another document, and shall be binding on the parties to the action, their officers, agents, servants, employees, and attorneys and on those persons in active concert or participation with them who receive actual notice of the injunction.

(d) **Motion to Dissolve**. A party against whom a temporary injunction has been granted may move to dissolve or modify it at any time. If a party moves to dissolve or modify, the motion shall be heard within 5 days after the movant applies for a hearing on the motion.

Rule 1.620 Receivers

(a) **Notice**. The provisions of rule 1.610 as to notice shall apply to applications for the appointment of receivers.

(b) **Report**. Every receiver shall file in the clerk's office a true and complete inventory under oath of the property coming under the receiver's control or possession under the receiver's appointment within 20 days after appointment. Every 3 months unless the court otherwise orders, the receiver shall file in the same office an inventory and account under oath of any additional property or effects which the receiver has discovered or which shall have come to the receiver's hands since appointment, and of the amount remaining in the hands of or invested by the receiver, and of the manner in which the same is secured or invested, stating the balance due from or to the receiver at the time of rendering the last account and the receipts and expenditures since that time. When a receiver neglects to file the inventory and account, the court shall enter an order requiring the receiver to file such inventory and account and to pay out of the receiver's own funds the expenses of the order and the proceedings thereon within not more than 20 days after being served with a copy of such order.

(c) **Bond**. The court may grant leave to put the bond of the receiver in suit against the sureties without notice to the sureties of the application for such leave.

Rule 1.625 Proceedings Against Surety on Judicial Bonds

When any rule or statute requires or permits giving of bond by a party in a judicial proceeding, the surety on the bond submits to the jurisdiction of the court when the bond is approved. The surety must furnish the address for the service of documents affecting the surety's liability on the bond to the officer to whom the bond is given at that time. The liability of the surety may be enforced on motion without the necessity of an independent action. The motion must be served on the surety at the address furnished to the officer. The surety must serve a response to the motion within 20 days after service of the motion, asserting any defenses in law or in fact. If the surety fails to serve a response within the time allowed, a default may be taken. If the surety serves a response, the issues raised must be decided by the court on reasonable notice to the parties. The right to jury trial shall not be abridged in any such proceedings.

Rule 1.630 Extraordinary Remedies

(a) **Applicability**. This rule applies to actions for the issuance of writs of mandamus, prohibition, quo warranto, and habeas corpus.
(b) **Initial Pleading**. The initial pleading must be a complaint. It must contain:
   (1) the facts on which the plaintiff relies for relief;
   (2) a request for the relief sought; and
   (3) if desired, argument in support of the complaint with citations of authority. The caption must show the action filed in the name of the plaintiff in all cases and not on the relation of the state. When the complaint seeks a writ directed to a lower court or to a governmental or administrative agency, a copy of as much of the record as is necessary to support the plaintiff's complaint must be attached.
(c) **Time**. A complaint must be filed within the time provided by law.
(d) **Process**. If the complaint shows a prima facie case for relief, the court must issue:
   (1) an order nisi in prohibition;
   (2) an alternative writ in mandamus that may incorporate the complaint by reference only;
   (3) a writ of quo warranto; or
   (4) a writ of habeas corpus.
   The writ must be served in the manner prescribed by law.
(e) **Response**. Defendant must respond to the writ as provided in rule 1.140, but the answer in quo warranto must show better title to the office when the writ seeks an adjudication of the right to an office held by the defendant.

Rule 1.650 Medical Malpractice Presuit Screening Rule

(a) **Scope of Rule**. This rule applies only to the procedures prescribed by section 766.106, Florida Statutes, for presuit screening of claims for medical malpractice.
(b) **Notice**.
   (1) Notice of intent to initiate litigation sent by certified mail to and received by any prospective defendant shall operate as notice to the person and any other prospective defendant who bears a legal relationship to the prospective defendant receiving the notice. The notice shall make the recipient a party to the proceeding under this rule.
   (2) The notice shall include the names and addresses of all other parties and shall be sent to each party.
   (3) The court shall decide the issue of receipt of notice when raised in a motion to dismiss or to abate an action for medical malpractice.
(c) **Discovery**.
   (1) *Types*. Upon receipt by a prospective defendant of a notice of intent to initiate litigation, the parties may obtain presuit screening discovery by one or more of the following methods: unsworn statements upon oral examination; production of documents or things; physical examinations; written questions; and unsworn statements of treating health care providers. Unless otherwise provided in this rule, the parties shall make discoverable information available without formal discovery. Evidence of failure to comply with this rule may be grounds for dismissal of claims or defenses ultimately asserted
   (2) *Procedures for Conducting*.

(A) Unsworn Statements. Any party may require other parties to appear for the taking of an unsworn statement. The statements shall only be used for the purpose of presuit screening and are not discoverable or admissible in any civil action for any purpose by any party. A party desiring to take the unsworn statement of any party shall give reasonable notice in writing to all parties. The notice shall state the time and place for taking the statement and the name and address of the party to be examined. Unless otherwise impractical, the examination of any party shall be done at the same time by all other parties. Any party may be represented by an attorney at the taking of an unsworn statement. Statements may be transcribed or electronically recorded, or audiovisually recorded. The taking of unsworn statements of minors is subject to the provisions of rule 1.310(b)(8). The taking of unsworn statements is subject to the provisions of rule 1.310(d) and may be terminated for abuses. If abuses occur, the abuses shall be evidence of failure of that party to comply with the good faith requirements of section 766.106, Florida Statutes.

(B) Documents or Things. At any time after receipt by a party of a notice of intent to initiate litigation, a party may request discoverable documents or things. The documents or things shall be produced at the expense of the requesting party within 20 days of the date of receipt of the request. A party is required to produce discoverable documents or things within that party's possession or control. Copies of documents produced in response to the request of any party shall be served on all other parties. The party serving the documents shall list the name and address of the parties upon whom the documents were served, the date of service, the manner of service, and the identity of the document served in the certificate of service. Failure of a party to comply with the above time limits shall not relieve that party of its obligation under the statute but shall be evidence of failure of that party to comply with the good faith requirements of section 766.106, Florida Statutes.

(C) Physical Examinations. Upon receipt by a party of a notice of intent to initiate litigation and within the presuit screening period, a party may require a claimant to submit to a physical examination. The party shall give reasonable notice in writing to all parties of the time and place of the examination. Unless otherwise impractical, a claimant shall be required to submit to only one examination on behalf of all parties. The practicality of a single examination shall be determined by the nature of the claimant's condition as it relates to the potential liability of each party. The report of examination shall be made available to all parties upon payment of the reasonable cost of reproduction. The report shall not be provided to any person not a party at any time. The report shall only be used for the purpose of presuit screening and the examining physician may not testify con-cerning the examination in any subsequent civil action. All requests for physical examinations or notices of unsworn statements shall be in writing and a copy served upon all parties. The requests or notices shall bear a certificate of service identifying the name and address of the person upon whom the request or notice is served, the date of the request or notice, and the manner of service. Any minor required to submit to examination pursuant to this rule shall have the right to be accompanied by a parent or guardian at all times during the examination, except upon a showing that the presence of a parent or guardian is likely to have a material, negative impact on the minor's examination.

(D) Written Questions. Any party may request answers to written questions, the number of which may not exceed 30, including subparts. The party to whom the written questions are directed shall respond within 20 days of receipt of the questions. Copies of the answers to the written questions shall be served on all other parties. The party serving the answer to the written questions shall list the name and address of the parties upon whom the answers to the written questions were served, the date of service, and the manner of service in the certificate of service. Failure of a party to comply with the above time limits shall not relieve that party of its obligation under the statute, but shall be evidence of failure of that party to comply with the good faith requirements of section 766.106, Florida Statutes.

(E) Unsworn Statements of Treating Healthcare Providers. A prospective defendant or his or her legal representative may also take unsworn statements of the claimant's treating healthcare providers. The statements must be limited to those areas that are potentially relevant to the claim of personal injury or wrongful death. Subject to the procedural requirements of paragraph (2)(A), a prospective defendant may take unsworn statements from claimant's treating health care providers. The statements shall only be used for the purpose of presuit screening and are not discoverable or admissible in any civil action for any purpose by any party. A party desiring to take the unsworn statement of treating healthcare providers shall give reasonable notice in writing to all parties. The notice shall state the time and place for taking the statement and the name and address of the treating healthcare provider to be examined. Unless otherwise impractical, the examination of any treating healthcare provider shall be done at the same time by all other parties. Any party may be represented by an attorney at the taking of an unsworn statement of treating healthcare providers. Statements may be transcribed or electronically recorded, or audiovisually recorded. The taking of unsworn statements of a treating healthcare provider is subject to the provisions of rule 1.310(d) and may be terminated for abuses. If abuses occur, the abuses shall be evidence of failure of that party to comply with the good faith requirements of section 766.106, Florida Statutes.

(3) *Work Product.* Work product generated by the presuit screening process that is subject to exclusion in a subsequent proceeding is limited to verbal or written communications that originate pursuant to the presuit screening process.

(d) **Time Requirements**.

(1) The notice of intent to initiate litigation shall be served by certified mail, return receipt requested, prior to the expiration of any applicable statute of limitations or statute of repose. If an extension has been granted under section 766.104(2), Florida Statutes, or by agreement of the parties, the notice shall be served within the extended period.

(2) The action may not be filed against any defendant until 90 days after the notice of intent to initiate litigation was mailed to that party. The action may be filed against any party at any time after the notice of intent to initiate litigation has been mailed after the claimant has received a written rejection of the claim from that party.

(3) To avoid being barred by the applicable statute of limitations, an action must be filed within 60 days or within the remainder of the time of the statute of limitations after the notice of intent to initiate litigation was received, whichever is longer, after the earliest of the following:

(A) The expiration of 90 days after the date of receipt of the notice of intent to initiate litigation.

(B) The expiration of 180 days after mailing of the notice of intent to initiate litigation if the claim is controlled by section 768.28(6)(a), Florida Statutes.

(C) Receipt by claimant of a written rejection of the claim.

(D) The expiration of any extension of the 90-day presuit screening period stipulated to by the parties in accordance with section 766.106(4), Florida Statutes.

Rule 1.700 Rules Common to Mediation and Arbitration

(a) **Referral by Presiding Judge or by Stipulation**. Except as hereinafter provided or as otherwise prohibited by law, the presiding judge may enter an order referring all or any part of a contested civil matter to mediation or arbitration. The parties to any contested civil matter may file a written stipulation to mediate or arbitrate any issue between them at any time. Such stipulation shall be incorporated into the order of referral.

(1) *Conference or Hearing Date.* Unless otherwise ordered by the court, the first mediation conference or arbitration hearing shall be held within 60 days of the order of referral.

(2) *Notice.* Within 15 days after the designation of the mediator or the arbitrator, the court or its designee, who may be the mediator or the chief arbitrator, shall notify the parties in writing of the date, time, and place of the conference or hearing unless the order of referral specifies the date, time, and place.

(b) **Motion to Dispense with Mediation and Arbitration**. A party may move, within 15 days after the order of referral, to dispense with mediation or arbitration, if:

(1) the issue to be considered has been previously mediated or arbitrated between the same parties pursuant to Florida law;

(2) the issue presents a question of law only;

(3) the order violates rule 1.710(b) or rule 1.800; or

(4) other good cause is shown.

(c) **Motion to Defer Mediation or Arbitration**. Within 15 days of the order of referral, any party may file a motion with the court to defer the proceeding. The movant shall set the motion to defer for hearing prior to the scheduled date for mediation or arbitration. Notice of the hearing shall be provided to all interested parties, including any mediator or arbitrator who has been appointed. The motion shall set forth, in detail, the facts and circumstances supporting the motion. Mediation or arbitration shall be tolled until disposition of the motion.

(d) **Disqualification of a Mediator or Arbitrator**. Any party may move to enter an order disqualifying a mediator or an arbitrator for good cause. If the court rules that a mediator or arbitrator is disqualified from hearing a case, an order shall be entered setting forth the name of a qualified replacement. Nothing in this provision shall preclude mediators or arbitrators from disqualifying them¬selves or refusing any assignment. The time for mediation or arbitration shall be tolled during any periods in which a motion to disqualify is pending.

Rule 1.710 Mediation Rules

(a) **Completion of Mediation**. Mediation shall be completed within 45 days of the first mediation conference unless extended by order of the court or by stipulation of the parties.

(b) **Exclusions from Mediation**. A civil action shall be ordered to mediation or mediation in conjunction with arbitration upon stipulation of the parties. A civil action may be ordered to mediation or mediation in conjunction with arbitration upon motion of any party or by the court, if the judge determines the action to be of such a nature that mediation could be of benefit to the litigants or the court. Under no circumstances may the following categories of actions be referred to mediation:
   (1) Bond estreatures.
   (2) Habeas corpus and extraordinary writs.
   (3) Bond validations.
   (4) Civil or criminal contempt.
   (5) Other matters as may be specified by administrative order of the chief judge in the circuit.

(c) **Discovery**. Unless stipulated by the parties or ordered by the court, the mediation process shall not suspend discovery.

Rule 1.720 Mediation Procedures

(a) **Interim or Emergency Relief**. A party may apply to the court for interim or emergency relief at any time. Mediation shall continue while such a motion is pending absent a contrary order of the court, or a decision of the mediator to adjourn pending disposition of the motion. Time for completing mediation shall be tolled during any periods when mediation is interrupted pending resolution of such a motion.

(b) **Appearance at Mediation**. Unless otherwise permitted by court order or stipulated by the parties in writing, a party is deemed to appear at a mediation conference if the following persons are physically present:
   (1) The party or a party representative having full authority to settle without further consultation; and
   (2) The party's counsel of record, if any; and
   (3) A representative of the insurance carrier for any insured party who is not such carrier's outside counsel and who has full authority to settle in an amount up to the amount of the plaintiff's last demand or policy limits, whichever is less, without further consultation.

(c) **Party Representative Having Full Authority to Settle**. A "party representative having full authority to settle" shall mean the final decision maker with respect to all issues presented by the case who has the legal capacity to execute a binding settlement agreement on behalf of the party. Nothing herein shall be deemed to require any party or party representative who appears at a mediation conference in compliance with this rule to enter into a settlement agreement.

(d) **Appearance by Public Entity**. If a party to mediation is a public entity required to operate in compliance with chapter 286, Florida Statutes, that party shall be deemed to appear at a mediation conference by the physical presence of a representative with full authority to negotiate on behalf of the entity and to recommend settlement to the appropriate decision-making body of the entity.

(e) **Certification of Authority**. Unless otherwise stipulated by the parties, each party, 10 days prior to appearing at a mediation conference, shall file with the court and serve all parties a written notice identifying the person or persons who will be attending the mediation conference as a party representative or as an insurance carrier representative, and confirming that those persons have the authority required by subdivision (b).

(f) **Sanctions for Failure to Appear**. If a party fails to appear at a duly noticed mediation conference without good cause, the court, upon motion, shall impose sanctions, including award of mediation fees, attorneys' fees, and costs, against the party failing to appear. The failure to file a confirmation of authority required under subdivision (e) above, or failure of the persons actually identified in the confirmation to appear at the mediation conference, shall create a rebuttable presumption of a failure to appear.

(g) **Adjournments**. The mediator may adjourn the mediation conference at any time and may set times for reconvening the adjourned conference notwithstanding rule 1.710(a). No further notification is required for parties present at the adjourned conference.

(h) **Counsel**. The mediator shall at all times be in control of the mediation and the procedures to be followed in the mediation. Counsel shall be permitted to communicate privately with their clients. In the discretion of the mediator and with the agreement of the parties, mediation may proceed in the absence of counsel unless otherwise ordered by the court.

(i) **Communication with Parties or Counsel**. The mediator may meet and consult privately with any party or parties or their counsel.

(j) **Appointment of the Mediator**.
  (1) Within 10 days of the order of referral, the parties may agree upon a stipulation with the court designating:
    (A) a certified mediator, other than a senior judge presiding over civil cases as a judge in that circuit; or
    (B) a mediator, other than a senior judge, who is not certified as a mediator but who, in the opinion of the parties and upon review by the presiding judge, is otherwise qualified by training or experience to mediate all or some of the issues in the particular case.
  (2) If the parties cannot agree upon a mediator within 10 days of the order of referral, the plaintiff or petitioner shall so notify the court within 10 days of the expiration of the period to agree on a mediator, and the court shall appoint a certified mediator selected by rotation or by such other procedures as may be adopted by administrative order of the chief judge in the circuit in which the action is pending. At the request of either party, the court shall appoint a certified circuit court mediator who is a member of The Florida Bar.
  (3) If a mediator agreed upon by the parties or appointed by a court cannot serve, a substitute mediator can be agreed upon or appointed in the same manner as the original mediator. A mediator shall not mediate a case assigned to another mediator without the agreement of the parties or approval of the court. A substitute mediator shall have the same qualifications as the original mediator.

(k) **Compensation of the Mediator**. The mediator may be compensated or uncompensated. When the mediator is compensated in whole or part by the parties, the presiding judge may determine the reasonableness of the fees charged by the mediator. In the absence of a written agreement providing for the mediator's compensation, the mediator shall be compensated at the hourly rate set by the presiding judge in the referral order. Where appropriate, each party shall pay a proportionate share of the total charges of the mediator. Parties may object to the rate of the mediator's compensation within 15 days of the order of referral by serving an objection on all other parties and the mediator.

Rule 1.730 Completion of Mediation

(a) **No Agreement**. If the parties do not reach an agreement as to any matter as a result of mediation, the mediator shall report the lack of an agreement to the court without comment or recommendation. With the consent of the parties, the mediator's report may also identify any pending motions or outstanding legal issues, discovery process, or other action by any party which, if resolved or completed, would facilitate the possibility of a settlement.

(b) **Agreement**. If a partial or final agreement is reached, it shall be reduced to writing and signed by the parties and their counsel, if any. The agreement shall be filed when required by law or with the parties' consent. A report of the agreement shall be submitted to the court or a stipulation of dismissal shall be filed. By stipulation of the parties, the agreement may be transcribed or electronically recorded. In such event, the transcript may be filed with the court. The mediator shall report the existence of the signed or transcribed agreement to the court without comment within 10 days thereof. No agreement under this rule shall be reported to the court except as provided herein.

(c) **Imposition of Sanctions**. In the event of any breach or failure to perform under the agreement, the court upon motion may impose sanctions, including costs, attorneys' fees, or other appropriate remedies including entry of judgment on the agreement.

Rule 1.750 County Court Actions

(a) **Applicability**. This rule applies to the mediation of county court matters and issues only and controls over conflicting provisions in rules 1.700, 1.710, 1.720, and 1.730.

(b) **Limitation on Referral to Mediation**. When a mediation program utilizing volunteer mediators is unavailable or otherwise inappropriate, county court matters may be referred to a mediator or mediation program which charges a fee. Such order of referral shall advise the parties that they may object to mediation on grounds of financial hardship or on any ground set forth in rule 1.700(b). If a party objects, mediation shall not be conducted until the court rules on the objection. The court may consider the amount in controversy, the objecting party's ability to pay, and any other pertinent information in determining the propriety of the referral. When appropriate, the court shall apportion mediation fees between the parties.

(c) **Scheduling**. In small claims actions, the mediator shall be appointed and the mediation conference held during or immediately after the pretrial conference unless otherwise ordered by the court. In no event shall the mediation conference be held more than 14 days after the pretrial conference.

(d) **Appointment of the Mediator**. In county court actions not subject to the Florida Small Claims Rules, rule 1.720(f) shall apply unless the case is sent to a mediation program provided at no cost to the parties.

(e) **Appearance at Mediation**. In small claims actions, an attorney may appear on behalf of a party at mediation provided that the attorney has full authority to settle without further consultation. Unless otherwise ordered by the court, a nonlawyer representative may appear on behalf of a party to a small claims mediation if the representative has the party's signed written authority to appear and has full authority to settle without further consultation. In either event, the party need not appear in person. In any other county court action, a party will be deemed to appear if the persons set forth in rule 1.720(b) are physically present.

(f) **Agreement**. Any agreements reached as a result of small claims mediation shall be written in the form of a stipulation. The stipulation may be entered as an order of the court.

Rule 1.800 Exclusions from Arbitration

A civil action shall be ordered to arbitration or arbitration in conjunction with mediation upon stipulation of the parties. A civil action may be ordered to arbitration or arbitration in conjunction with mediation upon motion of any party or by the court, if the judge determines the action to be of such a nature that arbitration could be of benefit to the litigants or the court. Under no circumstances may the following categories of actions be referred to arbitration:

(1) Bond estreatures.
(2) Habeas corpus or other extraordinary writs.
(3) Bond validations.
(4) Civil or criminal contempt.
(5) Such other matters as may be specified by order of the chief judge in the circuit.

Rule 1.810 Selection and Compensation of Arbitrators

(a) **Selection**. The chief judge of the circuit or a designee shall maintain a list of qualified persons who have agreed to serve as arbitrators. Cases assigned to arbitration shall be assigned to an arbitrator or to a panel of 3 arbitrators. The court shall determine the number of arbitrators and designate them within 15 days after service of the order of referral in the absence of an agreement by the parties. In the case of a panel, one of the arbitrators shall be appointed as the chief arbitrator. Where there is only one arbitrator, that person shall be the chief arbitrator.

(b) **Compensation**. The chief judge of each judicial circuit shall establish the compensation of arbitrators subject to the limitations in section 44.103(3), Florida Statutes.

Rule 1.820 Hearing Procedures for Non-Binding Arbitration

(a) **Authority of the Chief Arbitrator**. The chief arbitrator shall have authority to commence and adjourn the arbitration hearing and carry out other such duties as are prescribed by section 44.103, Florida Statutes. The chief arbitrator shall not have authority to hold any person in contempt or to in any way impose sanctions against any person.

(b) **Conduct of the Arbitration Hearing**.
   (1) The chief judge of each judicial circuit shall set procedures for determining the time and place of the arbitration hearing and may establish other procedures for the expeditious and orderly operation of the arbitration hearing to the extent such procedures are not in conflict with any rules of court.
   (2) Hearing procedures shall be included in the notice of arbitration hearing sent to the parties and arbitration panel.
   (3) Individual parties or authorized representatives of corporate parties shall attend the arbitration hearing unless excused in advance by the chief arbitrator for good cause shown.

(c) **Rules of Evidence**. The hearing shall be conducted informally. Presentation of testimony shall be kept to a minimum, and matters shall be presented to the arbitrator(s) primarily through the statements and arguments of counsel.

(d) **Orders**. The chief arbitrator may issue instructions as are necessary for the expeditious and orderly conduct of the hearing. The chief arbitrator's instructions are not appealable. Upon notice to all parties the chief arbitrator may apply to the presiding judge for orders directing compliance with such instructions. Instructions enforced by a court order are appealable as are other orders of the court.

(e) **Default of a Party**. When a party fails to appear at a hearing, the chief arbitrator may proceed with the hearing and the arbitration panel shall render a decision based upon the facts and circumstances as presented by the parties present.

(f) **Record and Transcript**. Any party may have a record and transcript made of the arbitration hearing at that party's expense.

(g) **Completion of the Arbitration Process**.
   (1) Arbitration shall be completed within 30 days of the first arbitration hearing unless extended by order of the court on motion of the chief arbitrator or of a party. No extension of time shall be for a period exceeding 60 days from the date of the first arbitration hearing.
   (2) Upon the completion of the arbitration process, the arbitrator(s) shall render a decision. In the case of a panel, a decision shall be final upon a majority vote of the panel.
   (3) Within 10 days of the final adjournment of the arbitration hearing, the arbitrator(s) shall notify the parties, in writing, of their decision. The arbitration decision may set forth the issues in controversy and the arbitrator('s)(s') conclusions and findings of fact and law. The arbitrator('s)(s') decision and the originals of any transcripts shall be sealed and filed with the clerk at the time the parties are notified of the decision.

(h) **Time for Filing Motion for Trial**. Any party may file a motion for trial. If a motion for trial is filed by any party, any party having a third-party claim at issue at the time of arbitration may file a motion for trial within 10 days of service of the first motion for trial. If a motion for trial is not made within 20 days of service on the parties of the decision, the decision shall be referred to the presiding judge, who shall enter such orders and judgments as may be required to carry out the terms of the decision as provided by section 44.103(5), Florida Statutes.

Rule 1.830 Voluntary Binding Arbitration

(a) **Absence of Party Agreement**.
   (1) Compensation. In the absence of an agreement by the parties as to compensation of the arbitrator(s), the court shall determine the amount of compensation subject to the provisions of section 44.104(3), Florida Statutes.
   (2) Hearing Procedures. Subject to these rules and section 44.104, Florida Statutes, the parties may, by written agreement before the hearing, establish the hearing procedures for voluntary binding arbitration. In the absence of such agreement, the court shall establish the hearing procedures.

(b) **Record and Transcript**. A record and transcript may be made of the arbitration hearing if requested by any party or at the direction of the chief arbitrator. The record and transcript may be used in subsequent legal proceedings subject to the Florida Rules of Evidence.

(c) **Arbitration Decision and Appeal**.

    (1) The arbitrator(s) shall serve the parties with notice of the decision and file the decision with the court within 10 days of the final adjournment of the arbitration hearing.

    (2) A voluntary binding arbitration decision may be appealed within 30 days after service of the decision on the parties. Appeal is limited to the grounds specified in section 44.104(10), Florida Statutes.

    (3) If no appeal is filed within the time period set out in subdivision (2) of this rule, the decision shall be referred to the presiding judge who shall enter such orders and judgments as required to carry out the terms of the decision as provided under section 44.104, Florida Statutes.

Rule 1.900 Forms

(a) **Process**. The following forms of process, notice of lis pendens, and notice of action are sufficient. Variations from the forms do not void process or notices that are otherwise sufficient.

(b) **Other Forms**. The other forms are sufficient for the matters that are covered by them. So long as the substance is expressed without prolixity, the forms may be varied to meet the facts of a particular case.

(c) **Formal Matters**. Captions, except for the designation of the document, are omitted from the forms. A general form of caption is the first form. Signatures are omitted from pleadings and motions.

Forms 1.901 through 1.999 Available Online

As a courtesy, we have made the official forms (1.901 through 1.999) available online at michlp.com/floridaforms.

Standard Interrogatory Form 1 - General Personal Injury Negligence - Interrogatories to Plaintiff

(If answering for another person or entity, answer with respect to that person or entity, unless otherwise stated.)

1. What is the name and address of the person answering these interrogatories, and, if applicable, the person's official position or relationship with the party to whom the interrogatories are directed?
2. List the names, business addresses, dates of employment, and rates of pay regarding all employers, including self-employment, for whom you have worked in the past 10 years.
3. List all former names and when you were known by those names. State all addresses where you have lived for the past 10 years, the dates you lived at each address, your Social Security number, your date of birth, and, if you are or have ever been married, the name of your spouse or spouses.
4. Do you wear glasses, contact lenses, or hearing aids? If so, who prescribed them, when were they prescribed, when were your eyes or ears last examined, and what is the name and address of the examiner?
5. Have you ever been convicted of a crime, other than any juvenile adjudication, which under the law under which you were convicted was punishable by death or imprisonment in excess of 1 year, or that involved dishonesty or a false statement regardless of the punishment? If so, state as to each conviction the specific crime and the date and place of conviction.
6. Were you suffering from physical infirmity, disability, or sickness at the time of the incident described in the complaint? If so, what was the nature of the infirmity, disability, or sickness?
7. Did you consume any alcoholic beverages or take any drugs or medications within 12 hours before the time of the incident described in the complaint? If so, state the type and amount of alcoholic beverages, drugs, or medication which were consumed, and when and where you consumed them.
8. Describe in detail how the incident described in the complaint happened, including all actions taken by you to prevent the incident.
9. Describe in detail each act or omission on the part of any party to this lawsuit that you contend constituted negligence that was a contributing legal cause of the incident in question.
10. Were you charged with any violation of law (including any regulations or ordinances) arising out of the incident described in the complaint? If so, what was the nature of the charge; what plea or answer, if any, did you enter to the charge; what court or agency heard the charge; was any written report prepared by anyone regarding this charge, and, if so, what is the name and address of the person or entity that prepared the report; do you have a copy of the report; and was the testimony at any trial, hearing, or other proceeding on the charge recorded in any manner, and, if so, what is the name and address of the person who recorded the testimony?
11. Describe each injury for which you are claiming damages in this case, specifying the part of your body that was injured, the nature of the injury, and, as to any injuries you contend are permanent, the effects on you that you claim are permanent.
12. List each item of expense or damage, other than loss of income or earning capacity, that you claim to have incurred as a result of the incident described in the complaint, giving for each item the date incurred, the name and business address of the person or entity to whom each was paid or is owed, and the goods or services for which each was incurred.
13. Do you contend that you have lost any income, benefits, or earning capacity in the past or future as a result of the incident described in the complaint? If so, state the nature of the income, benefits, or earning capacity, and the amount and the method that you used in computing the amount.
14. Has anything been paid or is anything payable from any third party for the damages listed in your answers to these interrogatories? If so, state the amounts paid or payable, the name and business address of the person or entity who paid or owes said amounts, and which of those third parties have or claim a right of subrogation.

15. List the names and business addresses of each physician who has treated or examined you, and each medical facility where you have received any treatment or examination for the injuries for which you seek damages in this case; and state as to each the date of treatment or examination and the injury or condition for which you were examined or treated.

16. List the names and business addresses of all other physicians, medical facilities, or other health care providers by whom or at which you have been examined or treated in the past 10 years; and state as to each the dates of examination or treatment and the condition or injury for which you were examined or treated.

17. List the names and addresses of all persons who are believed or known by you, your agents, or your attorneys to have any knowledge concerning any of the issues in this lawsuit; and specify the subject matter about which the witness has knowledge.

18. Have you heard or do you know about any statement or remark made by or on behalf of any party to this lawsuit, other than yourself, concerning any issue in this lawsuit? If so, state the name and address of each person who made the statement or statements, the name and address of each person who heard it, and the date, time, place, and substance of each statement.

19. State the name and address of every person known to you, your agents, or your attorneys, who has knowledge about, or possession, custody, or control of, any model, plat, map, drawing, audio recording, visual recording, audiovisual recording, or photograph pertaining to any fact or issue involved in this controversy; and describe as to each, what item such person has, the name and address of the person who took or prepared it, and the date it was taken or prepared.

20. Do you intend to call any expert witnesses at the trial of this case? If so, state as to each such witness the name and business address of the witness, the witness's qualifications as an expert, the subject matter upon which the witness is expected to testify, the substance of the facts and opinions to which the witness is expected to testify, and a summary of the grounds for each opinion.

21. Have you made an agreement with anyone that would limit that party's liability to anyone for any of the damages sued upon in this case? If so, state the terms of the agreement and the parties to it.

22. Please state if you have ever been a party, either plaintiff or defendant, in a lawsuit other than the present matter, and, if so, state whether you were plaintiff or defendant, the nature of the action, and the date and court in which such suit was filed.

Standard Interrogatory Form 2 - General Personal Injury Negligence - Interrogatories to Defendant

(If answering for another person or entity, answer with respect to that person or entity, unless otherwise stated.)

1. What is the name and address of the person answering these interrogatories, and, if applicable, the person's official position or relationship with the party to whom the interrogatories are directed?

2. List all former names and when you were known by those names. State all addresses where you have lived for the past 10 years, the dates you lived at each address, your Social Security number, and your date of birth.

3. Have you ever been convicted of a crime, other than any juvenile adjudication, which under the law under which you were convicted was punishable by death or imprisonment in excess of 1 year, or that involved dishonesty or a false statement regardless of the punishment? If so, state as to each conviction the specific crime and the date and place of conviction.

4. Describe any and all policies of insurance which you contend cover or may cover you for the allegations set forth in plaintiff's complaint, detailing as to such policies the name of the insurer, the number of the policy, the effective dates of the policy, the available limits of liability, and the name and address of the custodian of the policy.

5. Describe in detail how the incident described in the complaint happened, including all actions taken by you to prevent the incident.

6. Describe in detail each act or omission on the part of any party to this lawsuit that you contend constituted negligence that was a contributing legal cause of the incident in question.

7. State the facts upon which you rely for each affirmative defense in your answer.

8. Do you contend any person or entity other than you is, or may be, liable in whole or part for the claims asserted against you in this lawsuit? If so, state the full name and address of each such person or entity,

the legal basis for your contention, the facts or evidence upon which your contention is based, and whether or not you have notified each such person or entity of your contention.

9. Were you charged with any violation of law (including any regulations or ordinances) arising out of the incident described in the complaint? If so, what was the nature of the charge; what plea or answer, if any, did you enter to the charge; what court or agency heard the charge; was any written report prepared by anyone regarding the charge, and, if so, what is the name and address of the person or entity who prepared the report; do you have a copy of the report; and was the testimony at any trial, hearing, or other proceeding on the charge recorded in any manner, and, if so, what is the name and address of the person who recorded the testimony?

10. List the names and addresses of all persons who are believed or known by you, your agents, or your attorneys to have any knowledge concerning any of the issues in this lawsuit; and specify the subject matter about which the witness has knowledge.

11. Have you heard or do you know about any statement or remark made by or on behalf of any party to this lawsuit, other than yourself, concerning any issue in this lawsuit? If so, state the name and address of each person who made the statement or statements, the name and address of each person who heard it, and the date, time, place, and substance of each statement.

12. State the name and address of every person known to you, your agents, or your attorneys who has knowledge about, or possession, custody, or control of, any model, plat, map, drawing, audio recording, visual recording, audiovisual recording, or photograph pertaining to any fact or issue involved in this controversy; and describe as to each, what item such person has, the name and address of the person who took or prepared it, and the date it was taken or prepared.

13. Do you intend to call any expert witnesses at the trial of this case? If so, state as to each such witness the name and business address of the witness, the witness's qualifications as an expert, the subject matter upon which the witness is expected to testify, the substance of the facts and opinions to which the witness is expected to testify, and a summary of the grounds for each opinion.

14. Have you made an agreement with anyone that would limit that party's liability to anyone for any of the damages sued upon in this case? If so, state the terms of the agreement and the parties to it.

15. Please state if you have ever been a party, either plaintiff or defendant, in a lawsuit other than the present matter, and, if so, state whether you were plaintiff or defendant, the nature of the action, and the date and court in which such suit was filed.

Standard Interrogatory Form 3 - Medical Malpractice - Interrogatories to Plaintiff

(These interrogatories should be used in conjunction with the General Personal Injury Negligence Interrogatories to Plaintiff.)

23. Do you contend that you have experienced any injury or illness as a result of any negligence of this defendant? If so, state the date that each such injury occurred, a description of how the injury was caused, and the exact nature of each such injury.

24. What condition, symptom, or illness caused you to obtain medical care and treatment from this defendant?

25. Do you claim this defendant neglected to inform or instruct or warn you of any risk relating to your condition, care, or treatment? If so, state of what, in your opinion, the defendant failed to inform, instruct, or warn you.

26. If you contend that you were not properly informed by this defendant regarding the risk of the treatment or the procedure performed, state what alternative treatment or procedure, if any, you would have undergone had you been properly informed.

27. State the date and place and a description of each complaint for which you contend the defendant refused to attend or treat you.

28. State the date you became aware of the injuries sued on in this action, and describe in detail the circumstances under which you became aware of each such injury; state the date you became aware that the injuries sued on in this action were caused or may have been caused by medical negligence; and describe in detail the circumstances under which you became aware of the cause of said injuries.

29. State the name and address of every person or organization to whom you have given notice of the occurrence sued on in this case because you, your agents, or your attorneys believe that person or organization may be liable in whole or in part to you.

Standard Interrogatory Form 4 - Medical Malpractice - Interrogatories to Defendant

(These interrogatories should be used in conjunction with the General Personal Injury Negligence Interrogatories to Defendant.)

NOTE: When the word "Plaintiff" is mentioned, these interrogatories are directed to be answered regarding (name of plaintiff/patient).

16. Please give us your entire educational background, starting with your college education and chronologically indicating by date and place each school, college, course of study, title of seminars, length of study, and honors received by you up to the present time, including internships, residencies, degrees received, licenses earned or revoked, medical specialty training, board memberships, authorship of any books, articles, or texts, including the names of those writings and their location in medical journals, awards or honors received, and continuing medical education.

17. Please give us your entire professional background up to the present time, including dates of employment or association, the names of all physicians with whom you have practiced, the form of employment or business relationship such as whether by partnership, corporation, or sole proprietorship, and the dates of the relationships, including hospital staff privileges and positions, and teaching experience.

18. With respect to your office library or usual place of work, give us the name, author, name of publisher, and date of publication of every medical book or article, journal, or medical text to which you had access, which deals with the overall subject matter described in paragraph [whatever paragraph number that concerns negligence] of the complaint. (In lieu of answering this interrogatory you may allow plaintiff's counsel to inspect your library at a reasonable time.)

19. If you believe there was any risk to the treatment you rendered to the plaintiff, state the nature of all risks, including whether the risks were communicated to the plaintiff; when, where, and in what manner they were communicated; and whether any of the risks in fact occurred.

20. Tell us your experience in giving the kind of treatment or examination that you rendered to the plaintiff before it was given to the plaintiff, giving us such information as the approximate number of times you have given similar treatment or examinations, where the prior treatment or examinations took place, and the successful or unsuccessful nature of the outcome of that treatment or those examinations.

21. Please identify, with sufficient particularity to formulate the basis of a request to produce, all medical records of any kind of which you are aware which deal with the medical treatment or examinations furnished to the plaintiff at any time, whether by you or another person or persons.

22. Please state whether any claim for medical malpractice has ever been made against you alleging facts relating to the same or similar subject matter as this lawsuit, and, if so, state as to each such claim the names of the parties, the claim number, the date of the alleged incident, the ultimate disposition of the claim, and the name of your attorney, if any.

Standard Interrogatory Form 5 - Automobile Negligence - Interrogatories to Plaintiff

(These interrogatories should be used in conjunction with the General Personal Injury Negligence Interrogatories to Plaintiff.)

23. At the time of the incident described in the complaint, were you wearing a seat belt? If not, please state why not; where you were seated in the vehicle; and whether the vehicle was equipped with a seat belt that was operational and available for your use.

24. Did any mechanical defect in the motor vehicle in which you were riding at the time of the incident described in the complaint contribute to the incident? If so, describe the nature of the defect and how it contributed to the incident.

Standard Interrogatory Form 6 - Automobile Negligence - Interrogatories to Defendant

(These interrogatories should be used in conjunction with the General Personal Injury Negligence Interrogatories to Defendant.)

16. Do you wear glasses, contact lenses, or hearing aids? If so, who prescribed them, when were they prescribed, when were your eyes or ears last examined, and what is the name and address of the examiner?

17. Were you suffering from physical infirmity, disability, or sickness at the time of the incident described in the complaint? If so, what was the nature of the infirmity, disability, or sickness?
18. Did you consume any alcoholic beverages or take any drugs or medications within 12 hours before the time of the incident described in the complaint? If so, state the type and amount of alcoholic beverages, drugs, or medication which were consumed, and when and where you consumed them.
19. Did any mechanical defect in the motor vehicle in which you were riding at the time of the incident described in the complaint contribute to the incident? If so, describe the nature of the defect and how it contributed to the incident.
20. List the name and address of all persons, corporations, or entities who were registered title owners or who had ownership interest in, or right to control, the motor vehicle that the defendant driver was driving at the time of the incident described in the complaint; and describe both the nature of the ownership interest or right to control the vehicle, and the vehicle itself, including the make, model, year, and vehicle identification number.
21. At the time of the incident described in the complaint, did the driver of the vehicle described in your answer to the preceding interrogatory have permission to drive the vehicle? If so, state the names and addresses of all persons who have such permission.
22. At the time of the incident described in the complaint, was the defendant driver engaged in any mission or activity for any other person or entity, including any employer? If so, state the name and address of that person or entity and the nature of the mission or activity.
23. Was the motor vehicle that the defendant driver was driving at the time of the incident described in the complaint damaged in the incident, and, if so, what was the cost to repair the damage?

Statewide Uniform Guidelines for Taxation of Costs in Civil Actions

Purpose and Application. These guidelines are advisory only. The taxation of costs in any particular proceeding is within the broad discretion of the trial court. The trial court should exercise that discretion in a manner that is consistent with the policy of reducing the overall costs of litigation and of keeping such costs as low as justice will permit. With this goal in mind, the trial court should consider and reward utilization of innovative technologies by a party which subsequently minimizes costs and reduce the award when use of innovation technologies that were not used would have resulted in lowering costs. In addition, these guidelines are not intended to (1) limit the amount of costs recoverable under a contract or statute, or (2) prejudice the rights of any litigant objecting to an assessment of costs on the basis that the assessment is contrary to applicable substantive law.

Burden of Proof. Under these guidelines, it is the burden of the moving party to show that all requested costs were reasonably necessary either to defend or prosecute the case at the time the action precipitating the cost was taken.

I. Litigation Costs That Should Be Taxed.
    A. Depositions
        1. The original and one copy of the deposition and court reporter's per diem for all depositions.
        2. The original and/or one copy of the electronic deposition and the cost of the services of a technician for electronic depositions used at trial.
        3. Telephone toll and electronic conferencing charges for the conduct of telephone and electronic depositions.
    B. Documents and Exhibits
        1. The costs of copies of documents filed (in lieu of "actually cited") with the court, which are reasonably necessary to assist the court in reaching a conclusion.
        2. The costs of copies obtained in discovery, even if the copies were not used at trial.
    C. Expert Witnesses
        1. A reasonable fee for deposition and/or trial testimony, and the costs of preparation of any court ordered report.
    D. Witnesses
        1. Costs of subpoena, witness fee, and service of witnesses for deposition and/or trial.
    E. Court Reporting Costs Other than for Depositions
        1. Reasonable court reporter's per diem for the reporting of evidentiary hearings, trial and post-trial hearings.
    F. Reasonable Charges Incurred for Requiring Special Magistrates, Guardians Ad Litem, and Attorneys Ad Litem

II. Litigation Costs That May Be Taxed as Costs.
    A. Mediation Fees and Expenses
        1. Costs and fees of mediator.
    B. Reasonable Travel Expenses
        1. Reasonable travel expenses of expert when traveling in excess of 100 miles from the expert's principal place of business (not to include the expert's time).
        2. Reasonable travel expenses of witnesses.
    C. Electronic Discovery Expenses
        1. The cost of producing copies of relevant electronic media in response to a discovery request.
        2. The cost of converting electronically stored information to a reasonably usable format in response to a discovery request that seeks production in such format.

III. Litigation Costs That Should Not Be Taxed as Costs.
    A. The Cost of Long Distance Telephone Calls with Witnesses, both Expert and Non-Expert (including conferences concerning scheduling of depositions or requesting witnesses to attend trial)
    B. Any Expenses Relating to Consulting But Non-Testifying Experts

C. Cost Incurred in Connection with Any Matter Which Was Not Reasonably Calculated to Lead to the Discovery of Admissible Evidence

D. Travel Time

      1. Travel time of attorney(s).

      2. Travel time of expert(s).

E. Travel Expenses of Attorney(s)

F. The Cost of Privilege Review of Documents, including Electronically Stored Information.